# Inside Anorexia

*of related interest*

## In and Out of Anorexia
### The Story of the Client, the Therapist and the Process of Recovery
*Tammie Ronen and Ayelet*
ISBN 978 1 85302 990 5

## Anorexics on Anorexia
*Edited by Rosemary Shelley*
ISBN 978 1 85302 471 9

## Drawing from Within
### Using Art to Treat Eating Disorders
*Lisa D. Hinz*
ISBN 978 1 84310 822 1

## A Systemic Treatment of Bulimia Nervosa
### Women in Transition
*Carole Kayrooz*
*Foreword by a service user*
ISBN 978 1 85302 918 9

## Bulimia Nervosa
### A Cognitive Therapy Programme for Clients
*Myra Cooper, Gillian Todd and Adrian Wells*
ISBN 978 1 85302 717 8

## Touch and Go Joe
### An Adolescent's Experience of OCD
*Joe Wells*
*Foreword by Isobel Heyman*
ISBN 978 1 84310 391 2

## Helping Adolescents and Adults to Build Self-Esteem
### A Photocopiable Resource Book
*Deborah Plummer*
ISBN 978 1 84310 185 7

## Cutting it Out
### A Journey through Psychotherapy and Self-Harm
*Carolyn Smith*
*Foreword by Maggie Turp, Psychoanalytic Psychotherapist*
ISBN 978 1 84310 266 3

# Inside Anorexia
## The Experiences of Girls and their Families

*Christine Halse, Anne Honey,
and Desiree Boughtwood*

Jessica Kingsley Publishers
London and Philadelphia

First published in 2008
by Jessica Kingsley Publishers
116 Pentonville Road
London N1 9JB, UK
and
400 Market Street, Suite 400
Philadelphia, PA 19106, USA

www.jkp.com

**Library of Congress Cataloging in Publication Data**
A CIP catalog record for this book is available from the Library of Congress

**British Library Cataloguing in Publication Data**
Halse, Christine.
Inside anorexia : the experiences of girls and their families / Christine Halse, Anne Honey, and Desiree Boughtwood.
p. ; cm.
Includes bibliographical references.
ISBN 978-1-84310-597-8 (pbk. : alk. paper) 1. Anorexia in adolescence--Patients--Biography. 2. Anorexia in adolescence--Patients--Family relationships. 3. Teenage girls--Mental health. I. Honey, Anne. II. Boughtwood, Desiree. III. Title.
[DNLM: 1. Anorexia Nervosa--Case Reports. 2. Adolescent. WM 175 H196i 2008]
RJ399.A6H35 2008
362.196'85262--dc22

2007017529

ISBN 978 1 84310 597 8

Printed and bound in the United States by
Thomson-Shore, Inc.

*For girls and families living with anorexia nervosa*

# Contents

# Acknowledgements

Many people helped bring this book to fruition. The eight girls and their parents whose stories are the basis for the family biographies in this collection generously gave up their time by agreeing to be interviewed and to share their experiences of the personal complexity of living with anorexia nervosa.

The families represented in *Inside Anorexia* are only a small proportion of the girls, parents, and families who were interviewed as part of the Multiple Perspectives of Eating Disorders in Girls Project. We're grateful for the insights and help from all the families who so unselfishly shared their stories in the hope that others could benefit from them.

This book would not have been possible without the support and help of the dedicated team of doctors, nurses, health professionals, and administrative staff who provided us with encouragement and support, and facilitated our interviews with girls and their parents. They have become valued colleagues who gave us an insight into the professional challenges that clinicians face in working with the knotty problem of anorexia.

We are also especially grateful for the support from the members of our multidisciplinary International Advisory Panel. All members of the International Advisory Panel are renowned experts, scholars, or clinicians in their respective fields who brought to their advisory role a range of backgrounds and expertise in working with anorexia nervosa and with young people, particularly teenage girls and their families. The support and high quality advice and feedback from our International Advisory Panel have been invaluable in helping us present a broad, cross-disciplinary range of perspectives on anorexia. More often than not, members of our International Advisory Panel provided feedback and advice on our research and writing quickly and at very short notice. We are very appreciative of their generosity, time, and contribution. Full biographical details of the members of the International Advisory Panel are provided (see pp.165–9).

Special thanks are due to the many people who provided suggestions and comments on earlier drafts of the book or contributed in other ways. This group includes: Mary Boughtwood, who offered personal insights from her own experience on the issues that concern parents; Emma Cotter for her encouragement and work in developing the early drafts of each family's story; Sarah Debelle, who formatted the draft manuscript and gave us helpful feedback that challenged us to rethink aspects of what we'd written; Linda Gibson, who carefully transcribed our interviews with girls, their parents, and families; Lyn Honey, who read and provided helpful feedback on early drafts of the book; Cynthia Rankin for her help with conducting some of the background research; and Ramesh Vannitamby for medical advice on key issues.

This book would not have been possible without the patience and encouragement of our respective families, who unselfishly relieved us of other responsibilities while we were busy working and writing. In particular, Chris thanks Martin and Sarah for always being there. Anne thanks her husband Mark for providing practical and emotional support in myriad ways and her mother, Lyn, for encouragement and childcare beyond the call of duty. Desiree thanks the members of her family for their support, advice, and love.

We would also like to thank the Australian Research Council, the Centre for Digestive Diseases, particularly Drs Tom Borody and Michael Barrett, and the Children's Hospital Education Research Institute (CHERI) for their generous funding of the Multiple Perspectives of Eating Disorders in Girls Project. Thanks to this support, we were able to spend several years researching and writing about the experience and impact of anorexia nervosa amongst teenage girls, their parents, and their families.

# Introduction

Teenage girls have the highest incidence of anorexia nervosa of any group in society but anorexia is a perplexing problem for everyone involved. People with anorexia often do not acknowledge their condition and resist treatment; distressed parents and carers are torn between meeting their child's demands and following the advice of medical experts; and clinicians and health professionals often wrestle with the challenge of how best to manage this complex and potentially life-threatening problem.

*Inside Anorexia* is designed for people encountering anorexia for the first time or those who want factual information and an insight into the lived experience of girls suffering from anorexia and that of their families. The book has been written to meet the needs of people diagnosed with anorexia, their parents and families, and the increasing number of professionals from health, education, and social services who are encountering and dealing with teenage girls with anorexia and their families in professional practice.

*Inside Anorexia* brings together the stories of teenage girls with anorexia, their parents and families to provide an insight into the real-life experiences of those living with anorexia. These family biographies are combined with up-to-date information and research about anorexia from a variety of disciplines including health, medicine, psychology, and feminist and cultural studies. This information is based on critical analyses of the latest research as well as findings from the authors' own research, much of which has been published in more extended forms in international health, medical, and social science journals including *The European Eating Disorders Review, Eating Disorders: The Journal of Treatment and Prevention, Qualitative Health Research, Child: Care, Health and Development, Gender and Education,* and *The Journal of Community and Applied Social Psychology.*

The family biographies presented in *Inside Anorexia* are a small sample of the interviews collected as part of a large-scale study called Multiple

Perspectives of Eating Disorders in Girls, based in Sydney, Australia. The study involved in-depth life history interviews with adolescent girls diagnosed with anorexia and separate interviews with one or both of their parents and sometimes with other family members. At the time of interview, all girls were between the ages of 14 and 21 years, with an average age of 16 years and 3 months. All girls were being treated for anorexia in a hospital or on an outpatient basis and had been diagnosed between two weeks and seven years earlier. Reflecting the diversity of Australian society, families in the study represented a wide range of social and economic groups in terms of family income, place of residence, parental education, and occupation. Those who were interviewed came from a range of ethnicities including first and second generation migrant families where all or some family members came from China, India, or Italy. However, the bulk of interviewees were of Anglo-Australian descent. At the time of interview, none of the girls regarded themselves as "recovered," and their families and clinicians agreed with this view.

Each family member whose story is presented in *Inside Anorexia* was interviewed by one of the authors, sometimes on several occasions, and their individual stories have been woven into what we call "family biographies." The eight stories in this collection were chosen because they illustrate the diverse issues, experiences, and emotions of girls, parents, and families who are dealing with anorexia. These are tales of distress, resilience, courage, and hope.

Working with teenage girls with anorexia and their families at a time when they are highly stressed and vulnerable imposes significant ethical responsibilities on researchers. The ethical issues of working with girls with anorexia and their families are complex, and making sure that our research practice was sensitive to the circumstances of girls and their families has been an issue of concern that we have written about elsewhere.[1] As part of this broader ethical agenda we have kept in touch with the girls and families from the Multiple Perspectives of Eating Disorders in Girls project through an annual newsletter, and the girls and their parents whose family biographies appear in this book were invited to read a draft of their story. Several girls or their families have since contacted us and postscripts on their current circumstances follow their stories. We are humbly appreciative of the generosity and encouragement of the girls, their parents, and other family members. Without their support, this book would not have been possible. (All girls and their family members are identified by pseudonyms.)

This book has three unusual features. First, its organization is atypical. In most books on anorexia or other eating disorders the stories of people diagnosed with anorexia and their families are buried in a larger body of factual information. In such books, the stories serve as examples or case studies that are designed to illustrate general patterns. *Inside Anorexia* reverses this usual structure. In this book, the family biographies are the centerpiece and framework for presenting pertinent issues and information about anorexia. The purpose of this unusual approach is to make the important point—increasingly recognized in clinical and professional health practice—that the unique experiences and circumstances of individuals are the starting point for any discussion of anorexia amongst teenage girls and their families. This structure allows the book to be used by different readers in different ways: as a source of insight into the experiences of girls and their families; as a starting point for factual information on different perspectives of anorexia that direct the reader to influential research in the area; and as a collection of detailed case studies that can be used by health professionals, people with anorexia, and their families as a basis for discussion, debate, and analysis.

The second distinguishing feature of this book is its focus. While most books address the experience of anorexia from the perspective of recovered adult women looking back on their experiences, this book focuses on *teenage girls* who are *currently suffering* with anorexia *and* the experiences of their parents and families. In this way, *Inside Anorexia* offers an insight into the *actual* experience of anorexia *at the time* of the experience from the perspective of the family members who are touched whenever anorexia strikes a teenage daughter or sister in their family.

The third noteworthy feature of *Inside Anorexia* is its multidisciplinary orientation. Books about anorexia are generally based in a single discipline or even a strand within a discipline. In contrast, the information in *Inside Anorexia* draws on a range of disciplines, including health, medicine and psychology, feminist and cultural studies as well as original research findings from our own larger research project on the Multiple Perspectives of Eating Disorders in Girls. The aim of presenting a multidisciplinary approach in a single book is to give readers an overview of the different disciplinary perspectives on anorexia and guidance to further reading so they can avoid at the onset the burden of having to consult multiple references to get an insight into the perspectives of different experts on various aspects of anorexia.

A note on language: different disciplines have different views about the language that is best for accurately yet sensitively describing people diagnosed with anorexia nervosa. After much discussion and consultation, we have used the phrases "people diagnosed with anorexia" and, far less frequently, "people with anorexia." Our decision was driven by the recognition that language both describes *and* constructs the identity of what is being spoken about. At the same time, this choice recognizes that all of the girls whose stories are reported in *Inside Anorexia* were diagnosed with anorexia but some of them rejected this diagnosis *or* accepted their diagnosis but were reluctant to have a life without anorexia. Regardless of language, it should be noted that all the girls and parents described their experience of anorexia as causing distress.

# 1

# Living with Anorexia Nervosa

Anorexia nervosa is colloquially known simply as "anorexia" and is now the third most common chronic illness amongst teenage girls. Anorexia is notoriously difficult to manage and treat and it has an average duration of around six to seven years. For some people, however, anorexia can last a lifetime and cause extensive, ongoing physical, social, and psychological problems for them and their families. Many of these problems persist even when weight has been regained.

Anorexia generates a great deal of commentary in everyday life and is a persistent presence in popular culture. Newspapers and current affairs programs reproduce pictures of emaciated girls; popular magazines speculate whether thin celebrities have anorexia; and we have all heard thin people being described, sometimes with envy, as "anorexic." Being thin is just the tip of the iceberg for this extremely complex problem. There are many different theories, models, and perspectives on anorexia. This chapter provides an introductory overview of current knowledge and ideas about anorexia.

## What is anorexia?

The Latin term "anorexia nervosa" literally means nervous loss of appetite. In fact, the term is a misnomer because the rejection of food by people with anorexia has little to do with appetite. There is a wide range of theories and opinions about what anorexia actually is. These vary from a biological disease to a protest against the oppression of women in contemporary society, and almost everything in between. Medicine and the biosciences view anorexia as a physical problem, predisposition, or illness, while psychology and related disciplines regard anorexia as a consequence of poor self-esteem, body image distortion, a compulsive desire for thinness, or family dysfunction. In all cases, anorexia is considered to be a problem located within the individual. Some scholars have criticized this view of anorexia as too limited because it ignores the social and political context of anorexia. Feminist writers, for instance, have argued that anorexia is a consequence of contemporary social, cultural, and political circumstances. They have described anorexia as: an expression of social, cultural, political, and gender anxieties; a metaphor for sociocultural concerns about consumption, personal display, feminist politics, and individual competitiveness; a site of cultural and social oppression; and a form of resistance to the impositions of a patriarchal culture.[2-6]

While different disciplines see anorexia in different and sometimes competing ways, "anorexia nervosa" is a medical term and anorexia is diagnosed using medical criteria. The guidelines of the American Psychiatric Association in the current *Diagnostic and Statistical Manual of Mental Disorders* (*DSM-IV*) provide four medical criteria for a diagnosis of anorexia:

- refusal to maintain a minimum body weight of at least 85 percent of what would be expected for the person's age and height

- intense fear of gaining weight or becoming fat

- misperception of one's weight and shape, an overemphasis on weight or shape in self-evaluations or denial of the seriousness of low body weight

- cessation of menstruation (i.e. amenorrhea), although this criterion is not applied to girls below the age of puberty.[7]

The *DSM-IV* identifies two subtypes of anorexia nervosa. People diagnosed with "restrictor type" anorexia limit the food they eat and may exercise excessively. People who also regularly binge eat and/or purge by making themselves vomit or by taking large amounts of laxatives or diuretics are said to have "binge-eating/purging type" anorexia. Some people who are initially diagnosed with restrictor type anorexia later develop binge-eating/purging symptoms.

The *DSM-IV* describes two other eating disorders: bulimia nervosa (bulimia), and eating disorder not otherwise specified (EDNOS). People with bulimia have similar symptoms to those with binge-eating/purging type anorexia but they maintain their body weight at, or above, the minimum normal level. Some experts believe that there is little difference between bulimia and binge-eating/purging type anorexia apart from weight, but others see them as two completely separate conditions.[8,9] EDNOS refers to disorders of eating that do not fit the full criteria for anorexia or bulimia. People often move between diagnoses at different stages of their eating problem, for example from anorexia to bulimia or EDNOS.[10]

The *DSM-IV* criteria are controversial.[8,11] They have changed over time and are likely to continue to change as knowledge and understandings of anorexia evolve.[12] Some experts argue that the DSM criteria are too narrow and exclude some people who suffer from anorexia but do not demonstrate all symptoms.[8,12] For instance, the 85 percent weight limit has been criticized as arbitrary and difficult to apply to children and adolescents,[13] the menstruation criterion has been contested as not applicable in all cases of anorexia,[14,15] and fear of fat appears to be absent in some cultures amongst people who would otherwise be considered to have anorexia.[16]

## History of anorexia

The term "anorexia nervosa" was coined by Sir William Gull during the nineteenth century but the phenomenon of self-starvation has a long history. Cases of women voluntarily refusing food and becoming severely emaciated, even starving themselves to death, have been documented as far back as the fourth century. Around this time, Christian teachings began to emphasize the sacred, immortal soul as separate from the sensual, material body and taught that the body was a barrier to salvation. From that time until relatively recently, self-starvation had religious rather than medical meanings, and was variously interpreted as evidence of demonic possession or heresy or a demonstration of devotion, piety, and self-sacrifice.[17,18]

With the evolution of medicine and science during the seventeenth and eighteenth centuries, religion began to lose its authority to explain physical ailments and self-starvation was explained in medical terms. In 1689, Richard Morton published what is now considered the first medical description of anorexia, although it had little impact at the time. In 1873 two leading physicians, the Englishman Sir William Gull and the Frenchman Ernest-Charles Lasegue, independently published accounts of anorexia. While both are attributed with identifying anorexia as a modern medical concept, Gull's medical report focused on how the physician came to conclude that the condition involved "simple starvation" with no organic cause, while Lasegue's commentary focused on the psychological stages through which patient and family pass during the course of the disease.[18] Neither Lasegue nor Gull emphasized a preoccupation with body weight or fear of fatness even though these criteria are considered central features of anorexia today.

## How common is anorexia?

Historically, anorexia has been considered a problem restricted to affluent, Caucasian women in developed western countries,[18,19] but it is now clear that anorexia can strike people of any racial, ethnic, or socioeconomic background.[20,21] Estimates of how many people are affected by anorexia vary greatly. Caucasian women in western countries are the most well-studied group and estimates of lifetime prevalence for this group range from 1.4 percent to 4.3 percent.[22–24] The number of people with partial or intermittent symptoms of anorexia is even higher, with five to ten times as many females believed to engage in fasting, self-induced vomiting, and/or abuse of laxatives and diet pills.[25] Anorexia is far less common amongst men and boys, with around one-tenth as many males as females being diagnosed.[26]

## What causes anorexia?

There are many different theories about the causes (etiology) of anorexia, but there is insufficient research evidence to prove any theory categorically.[9] Different individual, environmental, or sociocultural factors have been identified as possibly playing a role in the development and maintenance of anorexia in some people. Yet the presence of these factors does not mean that someone will develop anorexia. Rather, it is generally accepted that a combination of multiple, diverse factors is involved in any case of anorexia and that these often come together in ways that are unique for each individual.[27,28]

In the following section we provide an overview of the factors most commonly considered to play a role in the development and maintenance of anorexia. These factors are clustered into two broad groups.

## Individual factors

The characteristics of individuals, including their biological and psychological make-up, are thought to play a role in anorexia.

### Biological factors

Some scientists suggest that anorexia has a physiological cause. For example, disturbances have been found in the hypothalamus, the part of the brain that controls processes such as food and water intake, digestion, and metabolism. Abnormalities in the levels and function of particular hormones such as insulin, growth hormone, and cortisol have been implicated, as has the activity of neurotransmitters such as serotonin.[29,30] As with other proposed risk factors, however, it is difficult to discern whether any biological abnormalities in people with anorexia are a cause of anorexia or a result of stress or starvation.

Research suggests that some people may have an inherited predisposition for anorexia because it often co-occurs in families, although the mechanisms of genetic transmission are unclear.[9,31,32] The strongest evidence of a genetic component is that identical twins (who share 100% of genes) of people with anorexia have a greater risk of developing anorexia than non-identical twins (who share, on average, 50% of genes).[30,33] Based on clinical samples, if one twin has anorexia there is still only around a 55 percent chance that their genetically identical twin will develop anorexia. The implication is that while genetic factors may create a vulnerability to anorexia, other factors are necessary for the development of anorexia.

### Psychological factors

Anorexia has been described as a pseudo-solution for emotional or identity problems and lack of self-esteem.[34,35] Focusing attention on weight and eating may give a sense of control that enables people with anorexia to avoid dealing with other painful issues.[9] It has also been proposed that other psychological factors may accompany the development and maintenance of anorexia. These include depression, anxiety, alexithymia (an inability to recognize emotion or differentiate between emotional and physical signals) and extreme sensitivity to certain emotions such as disgust and shame.[35]

A number of psychological traits have been observed in many people with anorexia.[36-38] These include perfectionism, rigidity, anxiety, obsessiveness, compulsiveness, and dissatisfied perfectionism where the person is unable to gain satisfaction from their achievements because they do not regard them as good enough.[9,35] When these are present in an extreme form they can constitute a psychiatric disorder, but their exact relationship to anorexia is unclear. In many cases, the traits are present before the anorexia and may be a factor in the development of anorexia,[39] or they may emerge at the same time as the anorexia or be a strategy to disguise other contributing problems such as poor self-concept and fear of inner emptiness or badness, as in the case of perfectionism.[40,41]

Different subtypes of anorexia have been associated with different personality types. Restricting anorexia has been linked with obsessional, inhibited, and compliant behaviors while binge/purge type anorexia is more commonly associated with impulsive and extroverted behaviors.[38]

Some researchers have identified a relationship between anorexia and adolescent development. If an adolescent lacks a strong sense of identity and self-worth, the demands of puberty may seem overwhelming and they may seek refuge in a rigid preoccupation with weight and food.[28] Alternatively, an adolescent may regress to childlike behaviors to avoid the fears and conflicts of growing up, including sexual maturity and taking on adult responsibilities.[42,43]

Adolescence is a transitional period that can be especially stressful for girls. They face increased expectations for autonomy and independence as well as the physical changes of puberty and menstruation that signal emerging sexuality and the move from childhood to adulthood. It has been suggested that experiences which cause feelings of sexual shame or disgust may play a part in the emergence of anorexia[44] and the increased body fat that occurs with puberty can also be experienced as negative and stressful in a fat-phobic society.[18]

Despite this association between anorexia and adolescent development, other factors appear necessary for the development of anorexia during adolescence. For example, stressful events may have a particularly strong impact during adolescence or the developmental demands of adolescence may be at odds with particular personality traits that make adolescents more vulnerable to anorexia.[28,45]

## Factors related to individual experiences, environments, and sociocultural context

The second group of factors thought to cause or contribute to anorexia are individuals' experiences in their immediate social and cultural environments. This group includes stressful events, activities, and occupations, the influence of family and peers, and broader features of the social and cultural context.

### Stressful experiences

Anorexia is often described as a way of coping with stressful experiences in life.[35,46] Traumatic experiences such as sexual, physical, or emotional abuse are sometimes thought to be involved in the development of anorexia.[47,48] Some theorists believe the abused person refocuses their attention on their weight and eating to escape intolerable feelings and to experience some sense of control, while others believe that victims strive for excessive thinness to escape the notice or desire of their abusers and/or potential abusers.[9,49,50]

Other severe stress factors like the death of a loved one or the break-up of an important relationship may be influential for some people, but everyday stressors and transitions such as moving house, changing schools, or studying for major exams can be contributing factors in the development of anorexia for vulnerable individuals.[51]

For some people, it is not particular events that are experienced as unbearably stressful but their life situations. For example, eating disorders amongst minority women have been described as a reaction to prevailing life conditions that they cannot change such as poverty, racism, class discrimination, and heterosexism.[50]

### Activities and occupations

Some people participate in activities and occupations where there is considerable pressure to perform and weight is considered to affect achievement. Some people have linked their anorexia with a desire to succeed in sport or to encouragement and pressure from their coach or team-mates to lose weight.[52] Researchers have identified a relationship between the incidence of anorexia and subcultures that revolve around activities that emphasize leanness or impose weight restrictions such as ballet and "thin-build sports" like gymnastics.[53-5] People involved in such pursuits may be at greater risk of anorexia because the activities focus on the body, food, and performance, and these attributes are privileged by members of the subculture. However, personal factors may also be involved. Personality traits often linked with anorexia, such as perfectionism, control, and obsessiveness, may be more common within these competitive occupations because they are the very qualities needed to succeed.[56]

## Families

Some researchers contend that families may be a cause or contributing factor in the development of anorexia.[57,58] This contention is based on clinical observations of apparently dysfunctional family patterns in reportedly typical "anorexic" families, and includes parental failure to encourage self-expression, lack of emotional engagement and openness, inflexibility, maternal over-involvement and enmeshment, critical and coercive interactions, intrusiveness, hostility, conflict avoidance, and unrealistically high parental expectations.[6,59,60] Similarly, the family therapy literature identifies high ethical codes of sacrifice and loyalty in families of people with anorexia but also indicates that these qualities can be oppressive and disempowering for people diagnosed with anorexia.[61] Anorexia has also been related to problems in early childhood such as insecure infant attachment and the mother's failure to respond appropriately to her young child's needs.[62] Others have suggested that anorexia can have a constructive function within the family, for example, by holding together a strained parental relationship.[60]

While families have an influence on their children and some people maintain that their family environment contributed to their anorexia,[51,63] this influence does not occur in predictable ways. Research has not proved that "anorexic" families are any more dysfunctional than "normal" families prior to the onset of the anorexia and apparent family dysfunction may be a result, rather than a cause, of the presence of anorexia.[9,64]

A familial emphasis on weight and shape has also been identified as having a possible role in the development and maintenance of anorexia: for example, when family members demonstrate concern about weight and dieting, criticize a daughter's body shape, or display prejudicial negative attitudes to fat people.[59,65] While families almost certainly play a part in transmitting cultural concerns about eating and body shape as well as attitudes to food, this is neither necessary nor sufficient for the development of anorexia.[9,66]

## Peers

Peers have an important influence during adolescence and can be a source for learning attitudes and behaviors.[9] Peers may model and encourage dieting or purging, promote a focus on physical appearance and thin bodies, or encourage competition to be thin.[67,68] Being rejected or bullied may affect an adolescent's self-esteem, behavior, and emotions, and young people may try to change their appearance to gain acceptance.[69] Negative comments and teasing about weight by peers have been linked to disordered eating[34,70,71] as have forms of sexual harassment including touching, inappropriate sexual comments, gestures, and behaviors such as boys' public ratings of girls' appearance. Such incidents can alienate girls from their bodies or encourage them to criticize and change their bodies to try to bolster their self-esteem.[72]

## Broader social and cultural factors

Broader sociocultural elements can play a key role in the development and maintenance of anorexia.[17] Popular wisdom has it that anorexia is becoming more common and is spreading to different social and cultural groups because thinner female bodies are being presented as the social ideal in western societies. Historically, however, self-starvation has flourished during periods of prosperity when food was abundant and when less repressive attitudes allowed women opportunities outside the home. It is unclear why this is so but it has been suggested that corpulence in women is valued at times when women's capacity to procure food and perpetuate the family is prized and thinness is valued when biological survival is not an issue and women are expected to engage in more aesthetic, spiritual, or intellectual pursuits.[17]

In today's world, thinness is not seen merely as a matter of looks or fashion. Governments are concerned about rising rates of obesity and an association between thinness and health is heavily promoted by industries, governments, education systems, and medical associations. While individuals are bombarded with messages about the importance of being thin, they are also part of a culture where pleasure-seeking and con-sumerism are heavily promoted. High calorie foods are inexpensive, widely available, and aggressively marketed.[73] When girls have linked their anorexia to sociocultural factors, they have emphasized the way that dif-ferent social messages and values conflict with one another.[74] Feminist scholars, however, contend that the patriarchal organization of contempo-rary society oppresses women and keeps them in an inferior social and economic position. In contrast to men, this scenario causes women to be defined by their bodies and leads them to use food restriction as a coping mechanism.[6,75]

In western societies, dieting and the desire to lose weight have become the norm even for women who are not overweight.[76] In societies where thinness is highly valued, the ability to lose weight and stay thin is often greeted with admiration and envy[52,77] and this occurs even when weight loss is seriously unhealthy.[9]

The mediating role of sociocultural factors is generally acknowledged but, as with all the risk factors associated with anorexia, the presence of these factors does not mean that anorexia is inevitable or even likely. Rather, the decisive element appears to be the way in which particular combinations of risk factors come together in each individual case.

## How is anorexia treated?

There are a number of different treatments for anorexia nervosa but there is limited evidence about which are the most effective.[78-80] Different treat-ments seem to be appropriate for different people depending on individual factors such as age, history, medical condition, and psychological state. Because anorexia is such a complex condition, a team approach to treat-ment is important[81] and the treating team may include a psychiatrist, pedia-trician (for children and adolescents), physician, dietician, psychologist, social worker, occupational therapist, physiotherapist, and nurses.

### Hospitalization

Hospitalization, sometimes necessary if someone is in medical danger,[81] usually emphasizes weight gain through supervised meals, nutritional supplements, and sometimes non-oral methods such as nasogastric tube feeding.[82] In the past, treatment was often seen as punitive. Today, hospitals generally use a lenient approach with positive behavioral programs that reward eating and weight gain with privileges such as day leave. In addition to weight gain and medical stabilization, hospitals try to help people diagnosed with anorexia establish more normal eating habits, such as eating a wider variety of foods,[83,84] and attend to their psychological issues and needs. The extent to which this is achieved varies[85,86] and hospital stays may be shorter than desirable because hospital treatment is expensive and limited by health insurance programs.[87] Even after hospitalization, people diagnosed with anorexia and their families need continuing support.[88]

### Day treatment
Some clinics offer the option of partial hospitalization or day programs so that participants can go home at night and on weekends. The goals and treatments are similar to full hospitalization and generally involve medical management, nursing, supported meals four to seven days per week, and participation in a variety of groups run by clinicians. Day programs may help people diagnosed with anorexia to transfer the skills they learn to everyday life more effectively because they are not fully removed from their families and normal environments.[89,90] Although these programs focus on developing normal eating habits, patients' eating is less closely supervised than for inpatients and people diagnosed with anorexia need to be motivated to participate and to be comfortable with group therapy because this is a primary form of treatment.[90,91] While partial hospitalization is not suitable for everybody, for some it may be a beneficial alternative to hospitalization or provide a helpful transition to outpatient care.

### Outpatient treatment
The majority of people with anorexia are treated in a hospital or clinic outpatient program or in the rooms of a medical specialist in eating disorders. Such programs usually involve medical check-ups and management, nutritional counseling, such as the development of food plans, and psychological treatments.[92]

## Psychological treatments

The aims of psychological treatments are to reduce the risk of harm due to anorexia, to reduce symptoms, encourage weight gain, and to aid psychological recovery. A range of different psychological treatments is available for people with anorexia, whether inpatient, outpatient, or day patient. Family therapy aims to address family problems using a variety of interventions and/or offers families and individuals strategies to cope with anorexia.[93] For adolescents with short-duration anorexia, family therapy is often recommended and can be particularly effective.[78,79,94,95]

For adolescents and adults, many other psychological treatments are available. Although people diagnosed with anorexia and their families might feel more comfortable with some psychological treatments than others, the evidence of their efficacy varies widely. The following examples are indicative of the wide range of treatments available:

- behavior therapy, cognitive behavior therapy, and cognitive analytic therapy use evidence and logic to distinguish between real and distorted beliefs around anorexic thinking and resultant behaviors[96]

- interpersonal therapy targets four areas linked to the trajectory and maintenance of anorexia, namely grief (when anorexia is associated with the loss of a person/relationship), interpersonal deficits (if a person is socially isolated or in a problematic relationship), interpersonal role disputes (conflict with a significant other), and role transition (a significant life change)[97]

- individual and family psychotherapy employs psychoanalytical theory to help people diagnosed with anorexia and families develop an understanding of and an explanation for their problems

- narrative therapy seeks to help individuals relinquish anorexia as the dominant storyline in their lives by finding other stories by which they can construct a strong sense of themselves[98]

- experiential nonverbal therapies such as dance movement and expressive art are used to express feelings and experiences.[78,99]

**Medicines and pharmacotherapy**

No medication has been found to be effective in treating the symptoms of anorexia itself but medication may help with some of the problems that accompany anorexia, such as depression and anxiety.[100,101] For instance, drugs such as selective serotonin reuptake inhibitors (SSRIs) may be prescribed to help patients with additional disorders or symptoms of affective and anxiety disorders, especially if these other conditions affect the treatment of anorexia.[102]

It is difficult to predict what particular treatment approach is best for any particular person with anorexia and there is a body of theory and clinical observation which argues that until someone diagnosed with anorexia is ready to get better, no treatment is likely to be of very great benefit.[85]

# Recovering from anorexia

### What is recovery?

There is no clear consensus about the definition of recovery.[95,103] At the most basic level, a person might be considered recovered if they no longer meet the *DSM-IV* diagnostic criteria for anorexia but this does not mean that there has been a return to full physical and mental health. They may still experience difficulty and distress about their bodies and food, have significant psychological and relationship problems, and be susceptible to relapse.[10,104,105] According to a five-year outcome study of 95 people with anorexia, only a little over half the number of people who no longer had diagnosable eating disorders could be described as recovered if these other issues were taken into account.[106]

Sometimes recovery is defined as a "good" outcome on a standardized scale.[107-9] Such scales take into account a range of features such as weight, menstruation, eating behaviors like dieting, vomiting, and laxative abuse, social relationships, and educational or occupational functioning. While these measures provide more information than the diagnostic criteria, they still define recovery from a clinical and medical standpoint. They have been criticized for incorrectly assuming there is a norm that can be applied to all individuals in all contexts and for failing to take into account the perspectives and experiences that people diagnosed with anorexia have of their own well-being.[110]

Some clinicians and researchers argue that the perceptions of people who have experienced anorexia are the most useful guide to understanding recovery because recovery may mean different things to different people. For some people diagnosed with anorexia, recovery may not have an endpoint but be an ongoing, non-linear process that may continue for years after a healthy weight is achieved.[95,110–12]

Research into the perspectives of people who have recovered from anorexia suggests that recovery is individual but involves several fundamental elements. People who have recovered from anorexia have described: abandoning obsessions with food and weight; believing they would never return to their old anorexic ways; critiquing social pressure to be thin; believing that their lives were meaningful and that they were worthwhile and integrated people; and not feeling socially isolated.[113] Recovery has also been described as a process of self-development that includes: acknowledging feelings, inner sensations and perceptions; maintaining a sense of self in relationships with others; and establishing control over uncomfortable emotions.[112] These understandings of recovery do not mention weight or menstruation and bear little resemblance to traditional, objective measures of physical recovery.

## How likely is recovery?

When only core symptoms such as weight, menstruation, and eating behaviors are considered, a large body of research indicates that about half of all patients with anorexia eventually recover, although this can take a number of years. Around one-third do reasonably well but still have some symptoms and about one-fifth do poorly, become chronically ill, or die from the physical complications of anorexia or by suicide.[114–16] The chances of recovery are more complex and less clear when psychological and social concerns are considered or when people who recover without the help of mainstream services are taken into account.[52,114]

Despite considerable research, no factors have been identified that consistently predict a good or poor outcome of anorexia.[116,117] Historical, clinical, and environmental characteristics do not predict how well an individual will recover.[109]

## Other approaches

There is little research into factors other than treatment in assisting people to recover from anorexia,[113] but people who have recovered from anorexia consistently emphasize the importance of factors outside of treatment.[63,118,119] In particular, they have reported the importance of supportive and empathetic relationships, whether with family members, friends, or others; the importance of making the conscious decision to recover and being ready to recover;[85,111] and sometimes spiritual support.[113] Even once the decision to recover is made, recovery is still a long, arduous journey and people who have lived through anorexia emphasize that recovery requires patience, determination, and persistence.[85,119]

# 2

# "The Best Anorexic"
## The Story of Angela, Maureen, Mike, Dan, and Martha

Angela is tired of her anorexia. Tired of the emptiness it leaves; tired of it consuming all her days; tired of its hold on her. The past six years have been a relentless series of long-term hospital admissions and Angela knows that life is passing her by. She's often been close to cardiac arrest and renal failure; her bone density is perilously low and her beautiful teeth—the result of extensive orthodontic work—are loose and rotting in her gums. She's 158 centimeters tall but she only weighs 38 kilos and there's a real concern that her heart will stop if her blood pressure drops. Angela turned 18 in hospital and celebrated her twentieth birthday in hospital. Her twenty-first birthday is in a few days and she's just been re-admitted to hospital.

Angela dreams of having a job, a social life, and a boyfriend. She talks longingly about getting married and having a baby but her physical capacity to realize these dreams is getting increasingly distant as each day passes. Her parents, Maureen and Mike, don't feel Angela *really* understands what anorexia is doing to her body or to the possibilities for her future. Simple things that most young people take for granted—studying, working, and socializing with friends—are no longer part of Angela's world.

Angela is the middle child of three children. She was a jovial, confident, and carefree teenager, the sort of popular girl who always had a steady stream of friends hanging around the house. The family lives on the grounds of the elite college where Mike coaches football. Maureen and Mike find living on campus a bit like "living in a goldfish bowl." Being so close to work means Mike is always on call and this eats into the time he

## Box 2.1    Physical Effects of Anorexia

Anorexia can cause a wide variety of physical problems due to low weight, malnutrition, and the use of unhealthy weight-loss strategies such as self-induced vomiting and laxative abuse.[8,120,121] These cause loss of fat, biochemical disturbances like dehydration and electrolyte imbalance, and reduced blood levels of most hormones. The physical manifestations of anorexia include:

- emaciation
- cessation of the menstrual cycle (amenorrhea)
- gastrointestinal problems such as constipation, bloating, and indigestion
- dry skin and thinning, brittle hair
- fine, downy hair growing on the face and arms (lanugo)
- poor blood circulation and cold or even blue hands and feet
- slow or irregular heartbeat (cardiac arrhythmia)
- low blood pressure and slow heart rate (hypotension and bradycardia)
- low body temperature
- tiredness, lack of energy, muscle weakness
- dizziness and fainting
- anemia
- abnormal electrolyte balance (often due to vomiting)
- dehydration
- damaged teeth (from vomiting or changes to the production of saliva)
- liver problems (e.g. decreased function, fatty liver)
- kidney problems (including increased risk of kidney stones)
- fluid retention causing swelling, especially of hands and feet (edema).

Most problems can be reversed when a normal weight is reached and maintained but there is a possibility of permanent physical damage including osteoporosis (brittle bones), low hormonal levels, and growth retardation, particularly for girls who develop anorexia before puberty. The most extreme physical problems are heart or kidney failure and these can be fatal.

can spend with his family, but there are compensations. The family likes their roomy residence and the children have free and easy access to everything in the college, including its well-endowed library and first-class sporting facilities.

Angela's school is within easy walking distance of her home. For Angela, school was always a routine part of everyday life—a necessary, daily event. She accepted it unquestioningly because school was what all kids do. Angela's favorite time was the long, hot summer holiday. Free from the grind of classes and homework, Angela would use the summer break as an opportunity to get slim and fit. She fantasized that if she worked *really* hard, she'd look *really* good. Then she'd attract the attention of the college boys when they returned from their summer break. *Then* they'd like her.

The year Angela turned 15 years old was different. This time, Mike remembers, Angela continued her holiday diet and exercise program even after the school term resumed and the cool autumn weather started to set in:

> She started swimming early in the morning—maybe 50 laps or so of the Olympic pool—and then she'd go to school. After school she'd run and then maybe do some more swimming each day. I think that's where it all sort of started. She got less and less body fat and it just evolved from that, I think.

At home, weight was never an issue and the family didn't even own a set of scales. Angela's mother, Maureen, remembers this changed when Angela decided to join her school rowing team. Then weight became all important:

> She was being weighed for regattas and they had to be over 45 kilos. Angela was about 52 or 51 kilos, and 50 kilos was the ideal kind of weight. But there was another girl who was coxing the eight. She was a little Asian girl and very slight. Angela thought she missed out on coxing the eight because she was too heavy. But she was such a fit little person. For any of the fitness runs they did at school for rowing, she beat all the rowers. So she was very fit but this made her more and more driven to get fit *and* thin.

Maureen and Mike realized that Angela had cut down on what she ate and was exercising more, but she was so fit and muscular that the negative physical effects weren't immediately obvious. Angela's school friends and sister, Martha, knew Angela had been vomiting after eating for a long time but her parents were unaware until Maureen caught Angela in the bathroom after dinner one night. Angela vehemently insisted this was a one-off event. Maureen sensed the conflation of symptoms but couldn't bring herself to admit that Angela's defensive explanation might not be true.

With time, however, Angela's skin became dryer and a fine down began to grow on her cheeks. Maureen was concerned and took Angela to see their family doctor. He seemed certain that he was dealing with a teenager who'd recently started menstruating and took it for granted that she had a hormonal imbalance. He ordered some tests and reassured Maureen and Mike that the problem could easily be managed. It wasn't until a day or two later that, early one morning, Angela crawled into Maureen and Mike's bed and confessed that she'd been vomiting regularly for months.

Maureen found the idea of vomiting alien and repulsive but she pushed her feelings aside—a solution was more important than the problem. Maureen and Angela talked about the options and together they decided to see a private eating disorders specialist. Maureen felt this decision was "almost like starting on the journey to get better." The specialist's initial prognosis was positive. Angela's anorexia was in its early days and she could recover in a year. However, confessing to her mother and seeing the eating disorders specialist didn't prod Angela to cut back on exercising or stop forcing herself to vomit every time she ate. Within weeks, Angela's heartbeat was so irregular that she was put under close medical supervision. Within two months, her condition had deteriorated so much that she needed to be monitored closely and was admitted to hospital as a day patient. Two weeks later, Angela's heartbeat was still so irregular that she was rushed to hospital as an emergency patient.

It would be nine months before Angela was discharged. Even in hospital, Angela couldn't abandon the behaviors that were now so ingrained they'd become more than a habit—they were a way of life. Angela insisted that "being with other anorexic girls made her worse" but Maureen and Mike suspect this was just an excuse. Because Angela worked furiously to subvert any help or intervention, her weight and health continued to go downhill. In part, Maureen explains, this was because Angela "was able to throw up everything and get rid of it even two hours after eating." Angela's doctors were at a loss and finally decided that she would be better off in a specialized psychiatric clinic for eating disorders. Maureen and Mike weren't relaxed about the idea. Having only just got to know the clinical team, learn the hospital routine, and reorganize life so they could visit, moving Angela meant having to go through the whole process again. However, these were secondary issues. Angela didn't want to move. She didn't trust herself in a different place: "I'll be in a room by myself down there. No one's going to stop me from doing things and these voices in my head will make me be sick." Maureen and Mike questioned the wisdom of moving Angela when she was so set against the idea.

---

### Box 2.2   Anorexia: Part of an Eating Continuum?

There is debate about whether anorexia is a part of an eating continuum or a discrete problem.[22] Advocates of the continuum model contend that eating behaviors in the general population exist along a continuum ranging from self-starvation (anorexia) to excessive over-indulgence (obesity)[123] and that the eating behaviors of anorexia are typical of a significant proportion of people in the population who are also concerned about their weight, have poor body image, diet continuously, and are afraid of becoming fat.[124] They argue that using psychiatric criteria to describe eating behaviors stigmatizes individuals whereas the continuum model situates people's struggles with food as the product of a society that celebrates thinness and condemns large people.[125,126]

In contrast, those who consider anorexia to be a distinct condition argue that anorexia becomes "the sole purpose" of life and is characterized by more complex psychiatric behaviors and a significantly higher mortality rate than amongst individuals engaging in "normal" dieting and food restriction.[127] In contrast to "normal" dieters, people with anorexia set very low weight goals but are rarely satisfied when these goals are reached and strive to decrease their weight further, despite negative physical side-effects. Based on clinical and psychometric indicators of low self-esteem, perfectionism, and depression, anorexia has also been identified as a distinct psychiatric condition.[128] Those who consider anorexia as a distinct condition also point out that the continuum model is not a helpful one for clinicians treating anorexia and its associated problems because it fails to differentiate between the different eating disorders identified by the *DSM-IV* and seen in clinical presentations.

Nevertheless, the transfer went ahead. As far as Angela was concerned, the only way to escape the clinic was by making sure she got so thin and sick that there'd be no option but to send her back to the hospital. By now, Angela had an extensive repertoire of strategies to undermine any effort to help her regain weight. It only took her two weeks before her condition had deteriorated so much that she was returned to the hospital as an emergency patient.

Although she was only 16 years old, Angela ended up in the adult psychiatric ward because there were no beds available in the adolescent ward. Angela figured this was better than the eating disorders clinic but she still hated it and pleaded and nagged the staff to move her to the adolescent ward. Maureen and Mike visited every day, sometimes twice a day, but Maureen remembers how difficult that phase was for everyone:

> It's a scary thing for parents when eight months before you've got a seemingly normal child, and then you find her in the adult psychiatric unit. It's terribly frightening for a 16-year-old who just thinks she's only got a problem with eating. She doesn't really quite understand that it's a mental illness too. That was incredibly difficult for us. They were really tough up there in the psychiatric ward…but that's what she needed. That was hard at first. But then she got sicker and sicker. They put a special nurse on and even then she was still doing the wrong thing. I remember begging the doctor, "Why can't you just put her to sleep and just put the weight on her?" It was just a horrible, horrible experience. I wouldn't wish it on my worst enemy. To watch someone you love going through such hell and being totally powerless. As a parent, you've been able to help them in primary school when it was easy to give them a cuddle and make them feel better, or to help them through their trials in junior high school when they hit the difficult patches of adolescence. But it's terrible when you become powerless to actually help them. That was really, really difficult. They were really difficult times.

By this stage, Angela was so critically ill that Maureen and Mike agreed to formally hand over authority to the medical team to make decisions about Angela's treatment and well-being at short notice. At the time, this seemed like the necessary and right thing to do but it meant that Maureen and Mike were no longer consulted about Angela's treatment. When they wanted to learn about her progress, they were invariably told to "ask Angela." However, Angela was a notoriously unreliable source for accurate updates. Maureen struggled with the lack of information but she was just as upset by the sudden change in her status from mother to "nobody."

Worn down by the multitude of issues surrounding Angela's long hospitalization, Maureen and Mike promised Angela an overseas trip with the family and students from Mike's college—providing she was well enough to be discharged. It was a seductive strategy that stirred Angela into action and she managed to boost her weight to 37.5 kilos. Although this was lower than desired, her doctors and parents felt it would be better for Angela's emotional well-being to be discharged and go overseas. The long-awaited trip went ahead but Maureen has mixed memories of that time. Traveling with Angela was demanding and difficult:

> We had a lovely time but she couldn't eat this or she couldn't have that. So I had to deal with restaurants and people asking, "Could you just put it in the grill?" "Do you have fish and salad?" Or trying to find soup places because she wouldn't have a sandwich. So we toured like that. It meant that we missed certain things because we had to search for the right place where Angela would have something to eat.

When Maureen and Mike returned home, they settled into a new domestic routine. The family was together again but Angela's illness dominated life. Maureen and Mike loved their daughter but they could never come to terms with some aspects of her eating disorder:

> She regurgitates her food constantly. She came out of hospital doing that. When we'd sit down to a meal, Angela would keep bringing it back up and chewing it and swallowing it. It used to go on for hours. *It's revolting.* I can't get used to that. It makes me feel sick. We live with that but it's not nice.

Angela found she couldn't just pick up life where she'd left it. After such a long period of isolation from the social world, Angela was a mere shell of her former self and the once bubbly, vivacious teenager was now subdued and reserved. The bonds that tied her to many of her friends had melted away and she was apprehensive about trying to reignite old associations:

> I was really quiet because I'd been in hospital for a year. I didn't know how to speak to anybody anymore, and I was scared of talking to them. They thought I didn't want to be their friend and so we weren't that close. I don't really keep in contact with them anymore.

Because Angela had missed a year of school, she had to re-enroll in a lower grade to catch up. Despite being anxious about getting to know people, Angela found that she fitted in easily and quickly established a new circle of friends. She attended her regular check-ups at the hospital and this ensured that she kept her weight relatively stable. This was good luck rather than a commitment to recovery because Angela doggedly ignored her parents' advice about what or how much she should eat and soon abandoned seeing the dietician and psychologist they'd organized.

The end of the year brought a fresh series of crises. Angela knew she had one more year of school left but it was painful knowing her former class was graduating and getting work or going to college. The old pattern of swinging between starving herself and vomiting after she ate re-emerged with a vengeance. By February, Angela's health had started to slide backwards and her weight had plummeted. Hospitalization looked likely. This was the last thing Angela wanted but this time she listened to Maureen and Mike's advice. She literally managed to "eat her way out" of the crisis by consuming enough cheese and yoghurt to put on four kilos in two weeks. Not only did she avoid another stint in hospital but she was so much fitter and more energetic that she was able to start rowing again. This turn of events was such a positive, promising step that Mike and Maureen hoped they'd finally seen the end of Angela's anorexia.

In Angela's memory, the following year stands out as an idyllic period—the sort of time she'd love to recapture. She had an active, happy social life and finally made friends with some of the boys at her father's college. Angela was determined to do well at school and she studied hard, sometimes as much as 12 hours a day. Her effort was excessive but it paid off and she did well enough in her final exams to get into her chosen college. During this period, Angela's weight remained relatively stable. She was still haunted by anorexic thoughts and desires but felt she had them "under control" because she didn't want to lose more weight.

The transition from leaving high school and going to college proved more difficult than she'd ever imagined. Angela felt lost on the large campus, her friends were studying elsewhere and the social life wasn't as active as she'd expected or wanted. In this environment, it was difficult to make new friends and to feel like she really belonged. She was lonely. Gradually, Angela slipped into a depressive hole and the old pattern of starving and purging re-emerged. As her weight dropped to a critical low, the effects of the starvation set in and Angela became increasingly angry, aggressive, and difficult to reason with. Maureen remembers the trauma of readmitting her to hospital again:

> Trying to talk to Angela was like trying to talk to a crazy woman. She couldn't rationally accept what was happening. She honestly believed that she was fine. Then you'd get a glimpse of the hell she was going through. She'd say, "I just want to die. I can't cope with this anymore. I don't want to live." And you'd *desperately* try to persuade her to think otherwise.
>
> I can remember being attacked by her. It was the night that we saw the surgeons and other doctors to work out how they were going to try and save her. She jumped up on her bed and demanded to know what we were talking about. I said, "You're going to die in a couple of days if they don't do something now. You're already hitting renal failure...we've signed papers so they can stitch the nasogastric tube into your nose." Angela got up and started punching me and screaming at me and saying that she hated me and that she would die hating me if I let them do it. That was terrible. I thought that if they don't save her the next day, she'll die hating me and that I won't be able to live with that. Those were our last parting words... It was awful. It was just horrendous.
>
> I expected the anger to subside after the surgery and general anesthetic but she wouldn't let herself sleep because then her heart rate and blood pressure and temperature would drop. Then the nurses would come in with another can of [liquid supplement]. So she made herself stay awake. She was like a raving lunatic. Her hair was falling out. What was left was all matted. Just a totally different person. I expected that once she had a sleep, things would be a bit clearer or she'd forget but there was just this hate, "Don't you speak to me, don't you come near me." She was very calm when she talked to [the doctors and nurses] and talked to her friends but with me it was all tears and anger... She was strapped to the bed and she was crying, crying, crying. All this anger over being refed...it was difficult to see her like that. Eventually, she put on weight and calmed down and was easier to talk to, but it was almost like treating a child.

By the time Angela reached 39 kilos and was discharged, it was too late to return to college and she was too absorbed in her anorexia to focus on studying. Instead, she spent the rest of the year "sitting at home, not doing anything." She had a second try at college the next year but she didn't have the physical or emotional reserves to cope. Eventually, Mike and Maureen supported her decision to drop out on the condition that she got a job, but Angela couldn't be rallied into action and the job never materialized. Instead, Angela secreted herself at home, becoming increasingly more withdrawn and isolated and days of doing nothing swelled into months.

---

## Box 2.3   Refeeding the Starving Body

Refeeding is required when a person is underweight, at risk of dying, or their long-term health is likely to be compromised without intervention. Parents often take responsibility for refeeding with food at home with considerable success. For example, in the "Maudsley Approach" to family therapy, refeeding takes place outside hospital and parents or carers take charge of meals and eating with the support of therapists.[92,129]

Refeeding can also take place in a hospital setting, particularly in cases of severe malnutrition. The aim of refeeding in hospital is to improve physical and emotional well-being, the ability to think clearly, and the capacity to benefit from talking and drug therapies to enable effective eating after discharge.[130,131]

### Methods of refeeding in a hospital setting

Most clinicians prefer to refeed through *supported meals*. These are nutritionally balanced meals and snacks where eating is supervised, supported, and encouraged by a staff member.[132] Someone on a program of supported meals is generally required to eat up to 3000 calories a day. This usually comprises three meals and three snacks and liquid supplements may also be prescribed.

*Nasogastric tube feeding* may be used when someone diagnosed with anorexia is in physical danger or is unable to gain weight using supported meals. A soft plastic tube is inserted through the nose and into the stomach and liquid food supplements are administered using a feeding pump, often during the night. Nasogastric tube feeding is usually conducted in conjunction with supported meals.

*Total parenteral nutrition* is rarely used and only with very chronic patients as a lifesaving measure. Patients are given nutrition through a catheter inserted into a large vein.

### Physical complications of refeeding

During refeeding in hospital, care has to be taken to avoid complications such as "refeeding syndrome." This involves a disturbance in the body's balance of electrolytes and is associated with delirium. Refeeding

---

syndrome is prevented by monitoring the blood levels of substances like potassium, calcium, magnesium, and phosphate, and supplements may be required so that the sudden intake of nutrients does not overwhelm the cardiovascular system and cause heart failure. The likelihood of complications is significantly reduced if food intake is increased gradually.[81,132,133]

Other physical effects of refeeding are less dangerous but can be unpleasant for patients. These include feeling full and bloated and experiencing stomach cramps, nausea, faintness, diarrhea, or constipation. Patients being refed can retain fluid, which can cause swelling, especially around the face and lower legs, and result in rapid, temporary weight gain, which patients may find alarming.[81,92,134] Graded exercise is sometimes recommended to combat the physical stress of refeeding and support rehabilitation of muscle.[135]

## Psychological experiences of refeeding

People diagnosed with anorexia can find the psychological effects of refeeding difficult and unpleasant, particularly if they disagree with the need to gain weight. After being on supported meals in hospital, some people can have difficulty regulating their own eating when they have to be independent and rely on their own resources.[136,137]

Nasogastric feeding also provokes ambivalence. Some people diagnosed with anorexia have described nasogastric feeding as a traumatic, negative experience but others have described it as a beneficial step to recovery.[82] For people diagnosed with anorexia, the meaning of nasogastric feeding is more complex than merely a physical experience and is seen in different ways by different people. It can be seen as a physical signifier of anorexia, a necessary and taken for granted medical intervention, a form of control and punishment by hospital staff, or a way of tricking the anorexia by disguising food intake.[82]

Individuals may experience some or all of these feelings and their response to refeeding may change over time. Individuals have more energy and can think more clearly after refeeding but they may feel that they have lost part of their identity and feel anxious or distressed about their larger bodies, especially if the psychological aspects of anorexia and refeeding have not been comprehensively addressed.[136]

Angela's troubles upset her sensitive, artistic older brother, Dan, who distanced himself from the daily dramas by spending more time with his friends and eventually moving out. It was a different story for Angela's sister, Martha. She was three years younger than Angela and still living at home. Martha was often on the receiving end when Angela's depression erupted in angry, violent outbursts. The resulting animosity caused a deep rift between the sisters. Maureen felt for her younger daughter:

> Every time we brought her to the hospital, Angela would scream abuse at her and be really horrible... In the end we said, "You know, it's not good for her and it would be best if she didn't visit." Martha felt that there was a lot of guilt being put on her... Angela would be pleasant to her one minute and then the next minute she'll be really nasty.

Maureen also remembers how Martha struggled to "cope with having to be a good girl while everyone else was fussing over Angela." Martha's response was to rebel. She started drinking, smoking, ignoring curfew, and took up with the "worst boy in the school." For the next couple of years, Maureen and Mike wrestled with the double burden of a daughter with anorexia and another suffering her own personal behavioral and psychological crises.

Martha's rebellious phase has since passed and the rift between the sisters has been patched up. Their relationship is now very different but Angela is uncertain about the reversal in sisterly roles her anorexia has caused:

> Martha's grown up and matured a lot. Now it's more like she's like my older sister and she's looking after me. It's really weird. I don't like that because it makes me feel inadequate. She's been really good but she's just trying to mother me now and I don't want that because it makes me look like a little girl. She used to look up to me [because] I'm three years older. She's going out and she's having so much fun. I want to be like that. But now she's doing all that and I'm the one who's at home doing nothing.

After six years of struggling with Angela's anorexia, Mike decided a lifestyle change was needed. He gave up his coaching at the college to take a job that gives him more time with the family. Mike finds Angela's anorexia difficult to comprehend and he's finally come to the conclusion that trying to tackle her resistance to food is doomed to fail. He's more comfortable with being affectionate and trying to encourage her in positive, supportive ways. Despite his resolve, the frustration of feeling powerless persists:

> She's much better than she was—early on she was very aggressive and angry and nasty. We're very close and we have a very good relationship but everything—your whole life—has to be dominated by what she

## Box 2.4　The Effect of Anorexia on Siblings

Having a sister or brother with a serious medical condition can be difficult and the emotional well-being, behavior, and academic performance of the well sibling can suffer.[138] Siblings have described anorexia as having a profound impact on their lives and causing intense and conflicted emotions.[139,140] Research into siblings' views has identified that siblings may:

- have little knowledge about anorexia and see it as attention-seeking and manipulative behavior
- compare their own bodies, eating habits, and willpower unfavorably to that of their sibling and this can have a negative impact on their self-esteem
- be scared their sibling will die or be ill forever
- feel a sense of loss, rejection, isolation, and abandonment if parents are focused on the child with anorexia, or feel hurt, resentful, frustrated, and overlooked, or as if they no longer occupy a special place in their parents' world
- experience their relationship with their sibling with anorexia as hostile or unpredictable and grieve for the lost relationship
- experience family life as filled with chaos, conflict, and tension and controlled by their sibling's anorexia
- feel responsible for looking after the sibling with anorexia yet feel powerless to help
- feel burdened by the unreasonable expectations of other people that they will always be tolerant, understanding, sensitive, selfless, and undemanding
- feel guilty about their feelings of anger, loss, resentment, and frustration
- struggle with personal emotions and issues because they keep their own feelings and problems to themselves.

Anorexia can have some positive effects for well siblings by making them more mature, tolerant, and empathetic or by enhancing understanding between family members.[139,141] Research suggests that it is helpful for parents to be sensitive to siblings' perceptions and attitudes and communicate effectively with them about the illness.[142,143] Formal programs to support well siblings of people with chronic and life-threatening illnesses may be helpful,[144] as well as support from other sources such as extended family, friends, school counselors, and family therapists.

wants. You just can't sit down and have a meal together because she's totally self-focused. You can't go somewhere because there's a fear it's going to be, "I've got to eat," "I've got to have my peas," or "I've got to have my carrots." Obviously to her it's all-important, but it's frustrating. You think, "Why do you have to do this? There's a bigger picture. There are bigger, more important things that you can be involved with or do with your life than worry about having a little bit of potato."

Maureen has kept her part-time job as a kindergarten teacher. She enjoys the work and the change in routine is a welcome reprieve from the daily grind at home. Besides, the extra money helps with the constant bills for doctors, psychologists, and other health professionals. At a personal level, however, the battle with Angela's anorexia has eroded her confidence in her abilities as a mother. Maureen feels she's "failed in some way" and begrudges having to mother Angela like she did 20 years ago: providing food and clothing; being constantly available and vigilant; taking Angela where she needs to go; making decisions for her. Worn down by years of trying to help Angela when she doesn't want to be helped, Maureen feels cheated of an adult relationship with her daughter at an age when Angela should be striking out on her own:

> The stress has been enormous. Dealing with doctors, going to appointments—dragging her to appointments she didn't want to go to and dealing with the stubbornness. It's been a long hard road.

Maureen and Mike tried family therapy but decided it wasn't for them. In hindsight, Maureen wonders whether she might have benefited from further professional advice. It might have helped her cope with Angela more effectively and alerted her to Martha's needs sooner. Nevertheless, Maureen and Mike haven't struggled alone. They both come from large families and have been able to call on their parents, brothers, and sisters for a helping hand. Mike's colleagues and students have been sympathetic and Maureen has drawn on a range of support:

> I've had family to talk to which has been good. You need that. I talk to the girls at work as well. They're always asking me how things are and it gets things off my chest—you can't talk to your own children about it on that level. And your husband. Sometimes your husband is really good to talk to about different things and he actually makes me think more clearly over certain situations. It's good to be able to talk to different people

because people in the community see eating disorders as a selfish act. They have very little understanding of it. So I hope when I talk to other people that they get some insight into… It's just like any other illness, you wouldn't choose to have it. And I've had good support from my staff and other mothers who have had daughters with eating disorders. We share similar problems, and it's good just to talk.

Maureen and Mike know there isn't "a magic cure" and, in many ways, they feel as if they are in mourning:

> I've lost the daughter I had. The anorexia took her. I think we've all kept trying and trying to get her back—back to that person we knew—but I don't know whether Angela will ever be the child she was. Perhaps that's a good thing, you know, in some ways. (Maureen)

Lately, however, Maureen and Mike are cautiously optimistic. Even though Angela's just been admitted to hospital for a fifth time, she seems calmer and more willing to listen and talk. Angela believes she's more motivated to recover than in the past:

> I always wanted to do well in everything I did so I had to do well at being anorexic. When I first got sick, I had to be the *best anorexic*. I would compete against all the other anorexic patients. People say, "Well, why don't you try to be the best at getting better?" It's not like that. But it's just dragged on for so long now, I just want it to finish. I've wasted so many years of my life with it. It's just holding me back. All my friends are moving forward and getting full-time jobs or in their last year of uni and I've done nothing. It's holding me back. I've matured. I've got the motivation now. I'm turning 21 next week but I've done nothing. I want a life and I want to get better and to be able to work and go out with friends and not stress about it. I just want to be happy again.

How things will go in the future is still uncertain. Nevertheless, Maureen and Mike have finally acknowledged that Angela's anorexia can't "run life as much as it has done." They'll always be by her side but the time has come for Angela to take charge of her future. The signs are promising and they look forward to a time when they will see Angela moving on and enjoying a productive life.

## Box 2.5   The Effect of Anorexia on Parents

Anorexia can affect parents' emotional well-being and their physical and mental health.[145-7] There are several features of anorexia that can cause parents particular anguish:

- *Impact on the child*—it is distressing for parents to witness their child's increasing emaciation and changes in behavior and personality, and to know how much the child is missing as a result of anorexia. Parents carry the burden of knowing that their child could remain chronically unwell, suffer permanent physical damage, or even die.

- *Uncertainty*—parents can receive conflicting, inaccurate, and even unhelpful advice and feel at a loss as to the best course of action. They can find that other people lack understanding or have misconceptions about anorexia and this can be isolating for parents.

- *Problems with treatment*—some parents have difficulty accessing appropriate and supportive treatment while other parents have experienced a number of failed treatments, felt excluded from their child's treatment, or encountered unhelpful health professionals.

- *Impact on the parent–child relationship*—many parents struggle to avoid upsetting their child but face ongoing conflict in trying to induce the child to eat more, exercise less, and attend treatment. Many have difficulty knowing when to be firm or flexible and relationships can become uneasy and lose their openness and spontaneity. Some adolescents with anorexia withdraw from one or both parents while others become increasingly dependent on a parent or parents.

- *Impact on home life*—parents may have less time for their partner, other children, and extended family. Friction and conflict can arise if other family members feel left out, do not understand anorexia, or disagree about how to manage the person diagnosed with anorexia. Living with erratic, unpredictable, or even violent or abusive behavior causes high stress levels in a family, and everyday routines such as shopping, cooking, and mealtimes can be disrupted or trigger tension and battles.

- *Impact on parents' own activities*—many parents feel that their whole lives are controlled by anorexia. Some have to give up activities they value like work, study, or sport because they are unable to leave their child alone or because caring for the child consumes their time and energy. Family leisure activities can become a thing of the past, particularly if they involve food or impinge on rigid anorexic routines.

Despite the difficulties, most parents remain committed and determined to help their child. Many parents consciously try to be optimistic and some find that their child's anorexia is the trigger for a renewal of their religious faith, increased sensitivity to the suffering of others, and better family relationships and communication.[148,149]

## Postscript

Angela's family has contacted us with an update. Seven years after being diagnosed with anorexia, Angela still has some issues with food but she is *much* better. She's moved to a new city, is holding down a good job, and is finally enjoying an independent life. As for Maureen and Mike, with all their children grown up and living away from home, they're fulfilling a long-held dream of living and working overseas.

# 3

# "Fat Attack"
## The Story of Carol, Lynne, John, Ben, and Shane

On a bright autumn day the sun floods into the airy lounge room. The house radiates the warm, relaxed feel of a home that's grown around its occupants and the living area is full of Lynne and John's three children. On the walls are drawings and paintings by their eldest child and only daughter, Carol. On the sideboard amidst the family photos and mementos of holidays together is a collection of football trophies and sporting banners won by Carol's two younger brothers.

Lynne grew up in an inner-city suburb. Although her parents passed away recently, she and her sister are close and know they can count on each other in a crisis. Lynne gave up her job as a food technologist after Carol was born but returned to work when all three children started school. She now teaches health at the local high school. John also grew up in a small, close family. He works in the food industry and has been with the same company for more than 30 years. The job involves long hours but he's been promoted often and is popular with his staff.

Lynne and John met at church when they were teenagers and married when Lynne was 19 years old. They're now in their mid-forties. As Lynne says, "We've grown up together." Both put great store on tradition, security, and family cohesion. John likes to plan for the future so he knows where he's going and how he's going to get there. He and Lynne have achieved most of the goals they set for themselves at the beginning of their married life. Now their children are older, they feel it's time to set new targets so that they can look forward to a comfortable retirement together.

Carol is a bright, vibrant 20-year-old who moves with the easy grace that comes from years of doing ballet. She's taller than both her parents but the family resemblance is clear. Carol has her father's blue eyes and mother's blonde hair. Today, there are no physical clues of Carol's long struggle with anorexia. Nevertheless, the dining room table is stacked with books on eating disorders—from hefty practitioners' aides to biographies, popular references, and even feminist and academic works. Carol and her parents are still searching for a "cause" in the hope of finding a definitive trigger that will make the trauma of the last few years comprehensible. They've spent hours hunting and trawling through these and other books, but the answer they're looking for still eludes them.

---

### Box 3.1   Searching for a Cause

The idea that finding the cause is necessary to solve a problem is widespread in research, clinical practice, and popular wisdom. This idea originated in the physical sciences and the "laws" of nature which presume that everything has a reason and that problems can be fixed by finding and repairing the breakdown.[150,151] In the biological sciences, problems are conceived of as relating to underlying flaws that can be diagnosed and eliminated.[152] Sigmund Freud, whose theories have influenced modern psychology, psychotherapy, and popular thinking, believed that emotional problems were caused by repressed, past experiences and feelings and that these could be examined, understood, and resolved if brought to a conscious level.[153]

While most medical and behavioral treatments for anorexia aim to address symptoms or maintaining factors, people search for causes to explain and understand experiences. A foundational principle of narrative therapy is that people make sense of their lives by mentally arranging past experiences into a sequence that provides a coherent story about themselves and their world. These stories provide a sense of meaning and continuity that can influence how people view themselves and their future actions.[98,152,154]

Many parents spend a great deal of time and energy trying to identify the causes of their child's anorexia to understand what has happened or is happening in the hope that this understanding will lead to a solution. They read a lot of literature and try to fit their memories of the past into different theories of anorexia. They note personality traits, behaviors, or events that appear to have contributed to their child's condition to identify those aspects that seem "typical" of anorexia and to reconcile those aspects that do not fit into their reading and understanding of eating disorders.

Those diagnosed with anorexia are less interested in searching for a cause, particularly if they do not acknowledge or want to change their

---

anorexia. From their perspective, there is no need to look for a cause if the anorexia is not seen as a defect that requires a cure. Those who describe their anorexia as a diet that went too far can recall *why* they decided to lose weight but not how or why the diet mutated into anorexia. Others explain their anorexia in terms consistent with eating disorders literature, such as genetics, low self-esteem, body image problems, perfectionism, issues with control, and problems with friends or boyfriends. These and more specific, complex explanations have often developed as a result of their personal research or through counseling.

While some individuals diagnosed with anorexia see the identification of underlying problems as important and beneficial to recovery, it can be annoying to have to deal with constant questions about the "cause" of their anorexia from clinicians, family members, and friends. On the other hand, the urge to search for a cause can lead to attributing blame and distract from the more important issue of recovery. Some accounts suggest that people diagnosed with anorexia can actively resist the search for a cause. For example, where individuals use anorexia as a coping strategy, searching for a cause can unmask issues that they are trying strenuously to avoid confronting.[155]

For some people, finding a cause for their anorexia may be the first step to addressing underlying problems and resolving the eating disorder. Making sense of the experience of anorexia by developing a plausible explanation may be part of the process of healing. For others, the search for a reasonable explanation may be futile and the best course of action may be to look toward solutions and focus on recovery.

Looking back, Carol believes her eating problems began as early as nine years of age. This was when she decided to stop eating red meat. Her decision wasn't shaped by any ethical or ideological concern. It was entirely aesthetic. She disliked the texture of meat and was repelled by the sight of steak oozing with red blood: "I just thought meat was gross. I think it was the blood that put me off it." A few years later, Carol found the physical changes of puberty just as off-putting:

> When I started developing I just hated it. Especially with being in ballet, it was really hard because I felt really uncomfortable not wearing a bra but even having to start wearing bras was uncomfortable. I just hated the whole changing of my body… I just didn't cope with it. I couldn't cope with my body changing.

Lynne had explained the physical changes that puberty would bring and Carol knew what to expect as she matured, but nothing could prepare her for what menstruation actually meant or how it felt. Her first period arrived when the family was traveling in the car on the way to their annual holidays. Carol was horrified by the idea of going through the same thing every month:

> Mom gave me this huge, thick pad and I cried the whole way to the holiday house. I cried for a whole week—just nonstop. I just couldn't handle it. I just kept thinking this is just complete hell. I don't—I can't—believe that women are putting up with this. Mom teaches it at school so she'd educated me, but I was just terrified about the whole process... I just hated getting my periods.

Carol and her father had a close, affectionate rapport during her childhood and early adolescence. They never talked much. In Carol's words, "It's a doing kind of relationship. Like we'll do things for each other but we don't actually talk to each other." Nevertheless, it was a demonstrative relationship characterized by lots of hugs and cuddles—at least until Carol started going through puberty. When puberty hit, Carol felt her father became increasingly distant and withdrawn and that the demonstrative bond they'd shared mysteriously seemed to stop. John has a different memory of the change in their relationship. He felt that with puberty, Carol became increasingly distant and "standoffish." She seemed overly sensitive and hostile about physical contact and any intrusion on her physical space. Eventually, even the smallest incident seemed to escalate into a major event. John remembers accidentally touching her on the behind while she was bending over in the kitchen unpacking the dishwasher. Carol's exaggerated overreaction made him feel like a child molester. After this occurrence, John went out of his way to avoid any physical contact with his only daughter.

Years later, after a therapy session with her psychologist, Carol wondered if her anorexia was an attempt to regain the physical connection of her prepubescent relationship with her father. Lynne has a different view. She points out that the change in Carol's relationship with her father was typical of most of Carol's relationships during this phase of her life: "The eating disorder really affected her relationship with lots of people…she just became so difficult, grizzly, and annoyed. We couldn't even hug her."

Carol enjoyed school. She had a wide circle of friends, was diligent with her school work and always did well. But school turned sour when Carol rebuffed the overtures of a boy who wanted to be her "boyfriend." Angry at being rejected, the boy enticed his friends to tease and taunt Carol and she unexpectedly found herself the target of snide comments and vicious jibes:

> I had braces at the time so they'd call me beaver and stuff like that, and they'd make really sexist jokes about me. About me being a woman and them being men… They turned a lot of the class against me for not liking him and saying that I was leading him on.

The harassment lasted for months and made Carol's life miserable. The daily bus rides to and from school were especially grueling and the persecution would leave Carol crying hot, angry tears. She wrote to the boy, begging him to control his friends and stop. Instead of getting a sympathetic hearing, the boy published her pleading letter on the internet and circulated the website address to her class mates.

Lynne feels the long drawn-out episode affected Carol so badly because she's such a gentle, sensitive person. Drawing on her reading about anorexia, Lynne describes Carol as "typical" of the sort of girl who might develop anorexia—a well-behaved perfectionist who is always cooperative and responsible, a determined high achiever. John has a different view. He believes Carol's eating problems were symptomatic of a deep-seated, long-term lack of self-confidence—the same insecurity and fragile self-esteem that many of her school teachers had commented on over the years. Even though Lynne and John disagree on this issue, they do agree that the episode with the boy had a harmful effect. In Lynne's words, "Her self-confidence was really knocked badly, so she decided that boys in general were too much trouble. It was a small event but it had quite a traumatic effect at that point in her life."

Carol concedes that the insults and taunts eroded her self-confidence. Despite being fit and slender, she became increasingly uncomfortable with the womanly shape she saw emerging in front of her eyes. She loathed her maturing body and was convinced that it was ugly. Unable to control the teasing at school, Carol's thoughts focused inward on herself and on

## Box 3.2  Coeducational versus Single-Sex Schools

Little is known about the incidence of diagnosed eating disorders in different types of schools but there is vigorous academic and media debate about whether single-sex or coeducational schools are more likely to foster eating disorders.

Studies that have compared the eating behaviors and attitudes of girls at single-sex and coeducational schools have produced contradictory findings. Huon[156] compared 311 students at two coeducational and two single-sex schools and found that girls in the coeducational schools were more likely to be seriously committed dieters than those attending the single-sex schools. Two comparative studies have found no differences in eating behaviors and attitudes between single-sex and coeducational schools.[157,158] In contrast, two studies have concluded that girls attending single-sex schools have more eating disorder symptoms. The first study compared 142 girls across two schools[159,160] and the second study was based on a sample of 647 university students who had attended different schools.[161] These findings challenge the popular wisdom that there is less pressure to be thin in single-sex schools and that girls in coeducational schools are more conscious of their body weight and shape because they want to be popular with the boys.

In fact, researchers have proposed that coeducational schools may encourage more flexible views of acceptable body types and that boys in a coeducational school provide a reality check because they do not find emaciation attractive. It has also been suggested that single-sex schools may provide more conflicting gender-role prescriptions for girls to be both ladylike and high achieving, and that this may contribute to disordered eating.[160,162]

While a student's school environment is likely to influence eating behaviors,[163] more research is required into the impact of specific school characteristics on the eating behaviors of students.[164] It is likely that the characteristics of individual schools, such as school policies, health education practices, school cultures, behavioral and achievement expectations, and attitudes of staff about weight and body shape, are more influential than school type.[165–8]

controlling her body and what she ate. She started weighing herself regularly—often dozens of times a day—and would stand in front of the bathroom mirror for hours composing long, detailed lists of imagined physical flaws she dreamed of changing:

I didn't even remember thinking, "Oh, I've got to lose weight. I've got to lose weight." It just happened. In the end, I was weighing myself all the time but I didn't actually think, "I'm fat." I don't actually remember thinking I was fat until I was deep into it and looking in the mirror and thinking, "Yeah, I'm fat." Your whole mind is distorted. You can't explain it but you look at yourself and you honestly think you look fat.

Even though Carol can't pinpoint making a conscious decision to lose weight, having stopped eating red meat long ago made it easy to stop eating other foods. She started by eliminating cakes and biscuits from her diet. Soon Carol started skipping meals and progressively gave up eating any dairy products and most proteins and carbohydrates. Almost imperceptibly, her resolve to reduce what she ate developed into a deep-seated fear of food. Even the *idea* of eating filled her with dread. Her heart would start racing, her palms would get sweaty, and she'd feel trapped and short of breath. It wasn't that Carol hated the *taste* of food. In her mind, even the *idea* of eating meant the start of an inevitable and doomed slide into fatness and ugliness. At the same time as she started culling food from her diet, Carol increased her exercise routine. Each day she'd walk the long route to and from school, thereby avoiding the harassment that accompanied the ride on the school bus.

For Carol, the slow drop of the numbers on the bathroom scales seemed to confirm that her efforts were working. There was further proof when, to Carol's delight, she stopped menstruating. In her heart, Carol knew that restricting eating so severely wasn't good for her health but she pushed her doubts aside. It was harder to resist self-starvation than to surrender to its incessant call.

At first, Carol managed to hide the fact that she was eating less and less. She wore five or six layers of clothes to conceal her emaciation and became adept at maintaining the appearance of eating. It was easy to skip breakfast and lunch because they were invariably eaten on the run or unmonitored. Dinnertime was trickier. When she came home late from ballet class, Carol would have her dinner alone and it often found its way into the rubbish bin. When the family ate together, Carol managed secretly to feed most of her dinner to the family dog. The dog relished the special treatment. Carol soon became his best friend but the dog quickly got very fat. Reflecting on her past, even Carol is surprised at the lengths she went to in order to disguise her food avoidance from her family. She chuckles as she

---

### Box 3.3   Body Image

The term "body image" was first used by psychologists in the 1950s and refers to the ways people perceive, think, and feel about their bodies.[169] One aspect of body image—body dissatisfaction—is a particular area of focus in eating disorders research. Clinicians describe body dissatisfaction as being experienced in three ways:

- distorted body image: "*I think I'm larger than I really am*"
- discrepancy from the ideal: "*I am larger than I would like to be*"
- negative feelings about the body: "*I don't like my body.*"[170,171]

Clinicians and researchers can assess body dissatisfaction by asking people to compare their bodies to what they see as an "ideal" body or to estimate the size of their bodies or body parts using computer images or silhouettes.[170,171]

Feminist scholars have criticized these techniques because they imply that any discomfort women feel about their bodies is an individual, internal problem. They argue that body image assessments reinforce women's negative feelings about their bodies and encourage them to focus on and evaluate their bodies.[172–4] Feminist scholars argue that a negative body image is a community pathology resulting from a society that defines women by their bodies, subjects women's bodies to intense scrutiny, and encourages women to diet, exercise, and even undergo cosmetic surgery to obtain the "right" body.

---

remembers funneling custard trifle into her socks and wrapping chocolate mousse in a serviette to shovel into the pockets of her jeans. Carol developed an expanding repertoire of excuses for refusing to eat particular foods. Lynne and John couldn't help but notice that she was increasingly irritable and that mealtimes were increasingly stressful.

Carol dreamed of becoming a professional ballet dancer and spent most afternoons and evenings taking ballet classes, rehearsing, or training in the gym. She successfully managed to juggle her ballet with her school commitments. Carol was also determined to do well academically and spent hours working on school assignments as well as rehearsing her dance routines. But as Carol's anorexia consolidated, she became increasingly critical of her performance. She complained about doing badly, of failing to meet the goals she'd set, and feeling inadequate. In an effort to

---

**Box 3.4  Anorexic Behaviors**

Anorexia can manifest itself in many different ways.[120,121,175] These include:

- severe reduction in the range and amount of food eaten
- vomiting after eating or bingeing
- taking weight-loss drugs like laxatives, diet pills, diuretics, and ipecac (induces vomiting)
- substitution of fat free gum (contains sorbitol which has a laxative effect) for food
- low calorie and low fat food and drinks
- excessive exercise
- rigid eating patterns
- insistence on cooking their own food
- refusing to eat but cooking for others
- deception to avoid eating
- disguising weight loss by wearing baggy clothes
- concealing weights in clothing or drinking water before being weighed.

---

redress her self-perceived failures, Carol intensified her energies on her schoolwork and ballet. Lynne and John were bewildered by her brutal self-criticism and zealous determination to do well. They knew Carol always got very good marks for everything she did. The problem was that Carol wasn't prepared to settle for just *very good*. She wanted to be the *very best*.

With her punishing schedule of dance classes, gym workouts, and studying, Carol escaped the taunts she'd suffered at school but it also meant that she let her friendships slide. She didn't have time for them anymore because any unaccounted time was spent carefully planning in minute detail her schedule for each day and following it with mathematical precision:

> I'd spend the night before I went to go to bed planning what I was going to eat the next day. And then each hour of the day I'd be waiting for the time slot that I'd put aside for that half a piece of apple or something like

that. So I'd have aims to get to. Like I would always be having these goals that I was meeting.

By the time Carol celebrated her sixteenth birthday, she'd developed crippling, chronic back pain. Sometimes, the aching was so intense that she couldn't move. At first, Lynne and John thought it was a ballet injury. Lynne took Carol to a succession of doctors who searched in vain for an explanation. Lynne trusted the health professionals to pursue the right leads but John became increasingly frustrated. He was always positive that Carol had an eating disorder:

> At the dinner table, the boys and I would be eating meat and normal stuff and she'd be picking on a few things, and we'd discuss what you should eat, what you shouldn't eat and all that sort of stuff [then] food became a taboo subject and as time went on you think—something is happening with this child. In her case, she had a bad back. She went through the whole gambit of medical tests to see what was wrong. Even with the specialists I said, "This girl has an eating problem." Yet they still pursued the back problem; the bone density problem; all sorts of tests. They were barking up the wrong tree. The amount of money we spent on medical costs was enormous [and] we knew she needed to be directed into an eating disorder help program. I said to Lynne, "This girl has an eating problem." I said that right from the word go.

After a year of ricocheting from doctor to doctor and irritated by the seemingly endless series of tests and investigations, John decided to give up banging his head against a brick wall. Frustrated and angry at the medical profession's failure to help, he effectively disengaged himself from any direct involvement in Carol's treatment.

Looking back, Carol acknowledges that her father was right and that her weight loss was the cause of her back problems: "I didn't have any muscle to hold my spine up anymore. It had all wasted away around my spine." Nevertheless, at the time Carol disguised her weight loss by drinking liters of water before being weighed by her doctor and by lying shamelessly when she saw the dietician. Raised in a religious household with a deep, personal commitment to her Christian faith, Carol didn't like herself when she lied. The constant subterfuge and deceit made her feel awkward and uncomfortable.

As Carol's self-starvation became more overt, she refused to eat anything except All-Bran cereal with water. Inevitably this meant that there were tears and tantrums at mealtimes but Carol's brothers no longer commented on her thinness or frugal eating. They worried their comments would cause a scene. Carol knew her behavior and emotions were getting out of control but she didn't have the inner resources to rein them in. She was so physically and emotionally invested in her anorexia that she couldn't bear the thought of changing.

The crisis came just before Carol's final exams at school when John's father died. Carol and her grandfather had always been very close and she was distraught at the sudden loss. The preceding years of intensive study and ballet practice, inadequate nutrition, and mental anguish finally caught up and Carol was so inconsolable that she couldn't sit her final exams. Lynne was alarmed when she discovered the real depths of Carol's misery:

> I found a note she'd written saying that she was deciding not to eat any longer. That it was all too much for her and life was too much. That's when I contacted her doctor and he got her into [the eating disorders unit] as quickly as he could and they sat her down—that unit is just brilliant—and they looked at her and looked at the information and they said, "Whatever else you've been told and whatever else you've been doing medically, that's important but we are letting you know now that you have an eating disorder, and you have to face it and that's it." The doctor was excellent. He was the first who just, sort of, took control.

The doctor explained to Carol that she was severely underweight and had low blood pressure and heart arrhythmia as well as amenorrhea. The diagnosis of anorexia nervosa put into words what Carol already knew but *hearing* the actual words was unexpected: "I had this fear all of a sudden because I realized that I was starting to die and that I was actually starting to kill myself." Lynne was relieved to have an authoritative explanation for the problems that had haunted them for so long. The diagnosis confirmed what John had been saying since the beginning but the news hit Lynne like a thunderbolt. Anorexia was much more difficult to come to terms with than a bad back. All sorts of future scenarios flashed through Lynne's mind. She cried uncontrollably. Worried about herself and desperate to calm her mother, Carol retreated to a nearby café with Lynne where she ordered a cheese sandwich and ate it without a murmur, as if to disprove the diagnosis to herself and her mother: "I remember being terrified of eating the sandwich. But I also remember thinking, 'Quick, I've got to eat something so I can calm my mom because she's crying and can't handle it.'"

Nevertheless, the diagnosis gave Carol something she'd missed as a result of all the chopping and changing between doctors—a designated physician to manage her case and oversee her well-being. The doctor gave Carol clear directions about what she should eat and how she should behave, but Carol ignored these instructions as soon as she walked out the door of the eating disorders unit. When she returned for a check-up a week later, Carol had lost another kilo. Her doctor wanted to admit her to hospital immediately and Carol was angry and resistant:

> I was just terrified that they'd make me fat. 'Cause they would. That's what they were going to do. They were going to feed me. That's all they wanted to fix. And I just didn't want it. I was quite happy with how I was. I didn't really care about being too thin.

Hospital would mean being by herself for Christmas and missing out on a long-awaited family trip interstate to spend Christmas with her grandmother. The only way Carol could visit her grandmother, the doctor explained, was if she stuck to a normal diet and drank liquid supplements at least twice a day.

Lynne and John laid down the law. If Carol didn't comply and stick to her end of the bargain then her holiday would be terminated and she'd be sent back home and admitted to hospital. Carol knew her parents never made empty threats. She also knew there'd be no skipping meals or hiding food at her grandmother's place. There everyone was expected to sit down to meals together and to eat what was served—no exceptions and no excuses. Carol remembers the visit vividly:

> I spent the next week up at my grandmother's house crying over each drink of supplement for half an hour, trying to drink it with a straw. When we came back I'd put on weight and that was devastating. Then I started to really get the taste of food back. It took like a month of Mom forcing me to drink this before I realized that actually I really loved that drink, and I actually really couldn't wait to have the next one [laughing]. My body was getting used to it I suppose. I adjusted to it. At the same time, I remember sitting there and Mom making an avocado sandwich. I think she just thought it was the best oil she could get into me. I took an hour to eat that sandwich. To this day, I can't eat avocado because it

caused me so much fear. I remember just hating the fact that I had to eat this food. Just hating the food and hating the *feeling* of it being in me.

When the family returned, Carol started a program of weekly visits to her doctor and regular sessions with a dietician and counselor. Carol's school assessment marks were good enough for her to be accepted into college without completing her final exams but she decided to take a year off. The idea of coping with college when she was just beginning to face the challenge of recovering from anorexia was too much. Carol took a break from dancing and began working at a local pizza shop. This was a new project for her and she embraced it with her typical thoroughness and attention to detail but without the obsession with which she'd tackled her ballet and school work. She was efficient and well-organized and was soon appointed manager, despite her youth and inexperience. Feeling more relaxed and confident, Carol also used this year to rebuild some of the broken relationships with some of her girlfriends from school.

Despite these successes, almost every meal resurrected Carol's fear of food and occasioned a painful panic attack. One of the recovery strategies she used was to introduce a new food into her diet every two months. It was always something substantial like bread, chicken, or milk. Slowly, this approach helped. Within 12 months, Carol felt she'd made enough progress to go to college. Lynne and John were confident she'd cope and supported her decision to leave home and move into student housing.

Two years after the elusive diagnosis, Carol seems well on the way to recovery. She's a leader in her peer group at college and is trying to be a little more forgiving and less demanding of herself. She makes a concerted effort to be more relaxed about completing her college assignments—resisting the need for them to be perfect in every respect and refusing to be driven by the urge to get the top mark in the class every time. Yet she still experiences what she calls "fat attacks." When a "fat attack" hits, Lynne pulls her back to reality by talking her through the crisis calmly, logically, and systematically:

> All of a sudden, she'd get upset and say, "I feel fat." She might have eaten something and she gets all guilty about it and she'll just start crying. We'll say, "What's wrong?" And she'll say, "I feel fat." It's a head thing. We just call it a "fat attack." She needs continual reinforcing and she needs it from all of us. She's not living at home now but she'll phone me in the middle of the night if one happens. In the last few weeks she hasn't had

one but before that she would probably have one every three weeks. She'd cry for a while and feel fat and she'd need someone to talk her through. You know, "You are a size 6. How can you be fat?" "But I feel bloated." "Well, you might feel bloated, it could be wind, you know." Her mind spins her into something and you've got to bring her back to reality by going through some questions with her... She couldn't trust her mind to do it. It seemed like she had to have someone else to help her control it at this stage so it was up to me till we could let her take control back over.

Carol doesn't believe that she's recovered but she is on the way and goes to regular counseling to help maintain this trajectory. Now that she feels she can understand her anorexia at an intellectual as well as emotional level, she's better able to analyze and come to terms with her feelings about food. At this stage, Carol feels she'll always feel anxious about eating and have difficulties with food. She likens recovering from anorexia to recovering from alcoholism—you are only recovered until the moment you backslide. However, accepting herself has lessened her dependence on anorexia:

Now the inner me is at peace with where I am. I find that inside of me I've got two different sections. There's a little ball inside of me that is my eating disorder now. It's probably only like the size of a tennis ball now. And it used to be all in me. It used to cover my body. As I'm getting better, my mindset's getting better. I'm really trying to fix the inner things and *then* work on the outside things. Then all the outside things don't seem so bad.

Her new understanding of herself has given Carol the strength she's needed to overcome her food phobias and to re-evaluate her priorities. Even though she once dreamed of being a ballet dancer, Carol's anorexia has made her rethink. She's hesitant about going into an occupation with a culture that is so focused on the body and where she might be vulnerable to disordered eating or relapsing into anorexia. Carol still loves dancing but she wants to do it for the fun and enjoyment and is examining different career options. She enjoys teaching Sunday school at her church and thinks teaching might be the right path for her.

Carol has regained the independence and self-confidence that the anorexia stole from her. She has a steady boyfriend who's been generous, supportive, and understanding. They've only been together for six months but Carol already knows they'll end up getting married. Her relationship with her father is now back on its old, comfortable footing and she's grateful to Lynne for her unwavering support even when times got tough. Carol describes her mother as her "best friend."

Lynne and John now feel the family can relax and joke with Carol without worrying that a random comment about food will cause a meltdown. Lynne and John's first priority has always been the needs of their three children but, now that Carol has passed the critical turning point, they're feeling more relaxed about the future. Now they feel that they have the time and freedom to look after each other, to enjoy life, and to plan for their own life together.

## Postscript

Carol has been in touch and tells us that her story has a happy ending. Her struggles with food are behind her, she has successfully completed college, and she did marry her boyfriend—they've just celebrated their first wedding anniversary.

# 4

# "If You're Not the Girl with Anorexia Then Who Are You?"

## The Story of Kate, Margie, Carl, Donna, Lucas, Joseph, and Reuben

Kate is a bright, capable, and artistic 14-year-old. Her sister Donna is ten years older and married a couple of years ago. Her three brothers Lucas, Joseph, and Reuben are 12, 10, and 8 years old. Kate's family lives in the city's outer suburbs on that invisible border where the urban sprawl starts to melt into farms and open countryside. It's a district with a peculiar aura of undecidedness—not city nor country and not quite sure how to define the something that lies in between.

Kate loves going to school. It's her "relief from everything." For a few short hours each day, Kate can lose herself in her schoolwork and the company of friends. She can escape the unrelenting burden of her anorexia. But school hasn't always been such a positive experience. Kate's tall and heavily built, just like her father. By Grade 5 (9–10 years old), she was already a head taller than everyone else in her class and weighed 65 kilos. Her mother, Margie, remembers those difficult final years in elementary school:

> She reached puberty when she was ten…she was large and because of the way she is built she had huge breasts… Their teacher in Year 5 had a thing about everybody putting their weight on the board [to illustrate] differences…that day really affected her. She came back distraught and she said, "I never actually realized I was actually a lot heavier than everybody else until it was written on the board." And then everybody started to tease her. I'd pick her up from school in the afternoon and she'd be in tears because she got teased and was being called "fatty" and "fatty

boomsticks" and all that sort of thing. Verbal bullying. It's just as bad as physical bullying.

Margie tried to console Kate by reminding her that this stage wouldn't last. Her body shape would change and the other children would grow. But Margie's concerned reassurances couldn't compensate for the hurt Kate felt when she was ridiculed about her size.

---

### Box 4.1    Schools and the Prevention of Anorexia

Schools are under increasing pressure from government, academics, and the popular press to stem the tide of eating disorders by instituting prevention programs.[176,177] Prevention programs aim to reduce the incidence of diagnosed eating disorders by decreasing rates of dieting, disordered eating behaviors (e.g. bingeing, fasting, vomiting), and preoccupation with body weight amongst students.[178] The effectiveness of prevention programs has been contested.[13,179] Some researchers have argued that it is better to invest in identifying students who are at risk of developing eating disorders as a result of dieting behaviors, body dissatisfaction, or other risk factors, while other researchers have queried the extent to which school-based prevention programs can counteract messages about exercising and thinness in schools and wider society.[180]

Very few prevention programs have been evaluated systematically and many of those that have been evaluated do not appear to have been particularly effective.[25,181] Even programs that have demonstrated some positive results have not isolated the essential elements for effectiveness.[166]

Nevertheless, school-based programs designed to prevent disordered eating attitudes and behaviors are still worthwhile because such behaviors are common in schools, particularly amongst girls, and can be harmful even if not symptomatic of a diagnosable eating disorder.[76,182] Experts in the field have identified the following guiding principles as helpful in planning and delivery of school prevention programs:

- Prevention programs should go beyond training people to adapt to noxious environments (e.g. resisting social pressure to be thin). More supportive social environments should be created by educating parents, teachers, and sports coaches, changing peer group norms, amending school curricula, and taking action to influence media images.[76,166] An important part of providing health-promoting environments is for school policies and practices to address body-based harassment, which includes weight-related teasing and sexual harassment.[70,180]

- Researchers caution that contemporary health ideologies can make a virtue of behaviors such as exercising and dieting which can be dangerous to good health when taken to excess.[163,183] Young people are vulnerable to such behaviors if they are part of a subculture that privileges thinness, such as ballet, dance, modeling, and some sports.

- Research suggests that it is ineffective to present information to students solely in lecture format.[71,182] It may be better to work with students in interactive groups, where students' own knowledge and experiences can be the basis for increased awareness, social support, and attitudinal change.[168]

- Caution needs to be exercised in presenting content during educational programs. Educating students about eating disorders may inadvertently introduce them to dangerous weight-loss tactics such as fasting, vomiting, and using laxatives[184] and learning about eating disorders may also suggest disordered eating as a strategy for expressing or getting attention for emotional distress.[185]

- Teaching students about "normal" weights and "healthy" weight management is a common prevention strategy but research suggests that it does not bring about healthier body images or behaviors.[25,182] It may also send undesirable messages that bodies must be closely monitored, managed, and controlled to conform to a narrow ideal.[70,168] A more helpful strategy is to promote healthy nutrition and exercise patterns for people of all weights while encouraging them to accept their own and others' diverse body shapes.[13,186]

- Teaching media literacy (i.e. the ability to assess media messages critically) may help students identify inaccurate images and stereotypes.[180] However, media literacy should go beyond a simplistic focus on thin models by attending to the many complex means by which the media reflects social cultures and influences how individuals experience their bodies and themselves.

- Experts who regard disordered eating as a way of coping with emotional problems and stress factors in life[187] argue that prevention programs should focus on helping students to cope more effectively by targeting factors like self-esteem, stress management, coping, assertiveness, social skills, empowerment, and stress factors during adolescence.[182,185,188]

Smarting from the ridicule of her peers, Kate was determined she wouldn't "go into high school fat." She cut out junk food and regularly cycled up and down the empty roads that snaked around the nearby houses. Midway through her first year of junior high, Kate was a bridesmaid at her sister Donna's wedding. For Kate, this was one of the happiest days in her life: "When I look back at my sister's wedding, that was when I was the perfect weight and I was happy and healthier. It's my goal to get back to there."

At the time, however, Kate had it fixed in her mind that life would be even better if she weighed just a little bit less and was just a little bit thinner. Gradually, she cut back on her food and ate smaller and smaller portions. Margie and Carl could see what was happening and worried. At school, Kate got by on water and not much else. Despite Margie's protests, she knew that on some days Kate "hardly had anything to eat." At the same time, Kate increased the time she spent exercising. She'd cycle for hours, do dozens of push-ups, and power-walked like she "had rockets on her shoes." If she lapsed with her diet by eating an ice-cream, she'd make up by riding the exercise bike for an hour. Exercise became an addiction. In Margie's words, "She obsessed over exercising. If it was raining and she couldn't get out to do exercise, she'd be hysterical. Absolutely hysterical." Even everyday activities mutated into a form of exercise designed to burn calories:

> She stands up all the time. Even to do her homework…she stands up on the bed to do her homework. You can never, never ever get her to do her homework sitting down. She read that in a magazine. It said you burn more calories standing than if you sit down [laughter]. (Margie)

Margie and Carl were troubled by Kate's unexpected drive to lose weight but rationalized that everything would be all right if they could just get her to eat. In hindsight, Margie admits this was a forlorn hope:

> You try to feed them up because you just don't want to admit it. And then you look at them one day and you think, "My god—a skeleton." She just looked sick. She'd lost too much weight. She turned sideways and her bones were sticking out. You think it's not going to happen to your child…you just think, "Oh, just give them more for dinner or more for breakfast and that'll fix it." But it doesn't.

At the same time, a series of unsettling compulsions emerged. Kate barely ate anything but she was constantly preoccupied with food. She spent hours each day cooking for the family.

> She would cook these beautiful cakes and muffins. We had muffins coming out of our ears, but she wouldn't eat them, and she'd make the lunches for her brothers. She'd insist, "I'll do this for them, I'll get their drinks." She'd be trying to control what they were eating at lunchtime. It was like the anorexia was saying, "Oh well, I'm making these sandwiches so I'm still controlling the food."

Kate was so engrossed with the idea of food that she'd meddle in the kitchen and get under Margie's feet when she was cooking. She'd stand in front of the oven for hours without moving or talking—just watching the dinner cook. Kate was such a nuisance in the tiny space that she was banned from entering the kitchen while meals were being prepared but this didn't deter her. Kate just redirected her energies to contriving ostensibly urgent reasons to be in the kitchen when cooking was happening: the need to phone a friend, to ask a question about homework, to get a drink of water.

One of Kate's other obsessions is counting. She counts anything and everything: the seconds ticking away on the old hallway clock, the number of steps she takes, the cars driving past the house. Sometimes she doesn't need to count *something*. She just counts. The monotonous, rhythmic sound of counting somehow seems to soothe her.

She's also preoccupied with neatness. Margie used to be particular about keeping the house orderly but three messy sons cured her devotion to neatness. Now it's Kate who's fanatical about keeping the house tidy. Everything in her bedroom has its place: her bed is always made before she goes to school, the pens and pencils are tidily arranged in even rows on her desk, and her clothes are always neatly folded and in her wardrobe. Kate has extended her compulsion for tidiness to her three brothers. She constantly tidies up after the boys, nagging them not to make a mess and harassing them to tidy their toys and keep their Lego and games neatly organized when they play:

> She drives her brothers up the wall. They'll be sitting on the lounge and she says, "Get up, get up," and straightens up all the cushions and the covers. And they say, "Oh, just go away, leave us alone." Then she drags

them off the lounge to try and get it all tidied up. And then she just nags, "You sit there and don't move!" She tries to control them through that. (Margie)

Her other compulsion is all-consuming. She's held captive by an uncontrollable urge to keep the living room floors spotlessly clean. She'll go to elaborate lengths to vacuum the wooden floors but her passion to clean doesn't bring her any contentment:

> She's obsessed with the vacuuming because the dog sheds its hair and we've got wooden floors downstairs. She has to vacuum every day and if it's not done it's a disaster. She's hysterical. She started on about the vacuuming this morning as soon as she got up. She said, "Are you vacuuming today?" And I said, "I can't do it and you're not going to." She got herself hysterical. If she can't vacuum, she'll be there with the broom for an hour. And she goes over the same spot a couple of times. So where it would only take me five minutes to sweep but it takes her an hour…then she'll be on the ground to get the dirt and the dog hair off with a towel or a tea towel. She'll be on hands and knees wiping even though there's nothing on the floor. (Margie)

The family's dog, George, has become one of Kate's victims. The large St Bernard seems to fill up any space and the dog hair on the floor is a constant reminder of his presence. Margie laughs as she remembers Kate's battles to control George:

> Because we've got wooden floors, every time George walks across the floor she says, "Get out of here, George," and his ears go back and you can see him think, "What are you yelling at me for?" She can't stand the dog hair on the floor. She blocks the lounge room and the dining room off with the dining room chairs [laughter] and closes the shutters to the kitchen and dining room so he can't get through 'cause he's too big. She yells at him and then she'll come out and say, "Oh, I'm so sorry George." He's so confused. He sort of looks at you as if to say, "I haven't done anything." It's just because he sheds his hair. As soon as he hears her come in, he just takes off into another room. The dog gets *very* stressed. He does. I'm not joking. The first time she started, he actually lost about four kilos, the vet said.

Kate's teachers also began expressing concern about her weight loss and behavior. Kate would fall asleep in class and was so weak she could hardly lift her school bag. It was a neighbor who first mentioned the word anorexia. She saw in Kate's emaciation and compulsive behaviors the same symptoms she'd seen in her nephew during his battle with anorexia. Difficult as Margie and Carl found the idea, everything suddenly seemed to fall into place.

Kate dutifully accompanied Margie to see a doctor who referred Kate to a dietician. Kate decided that seeing the dietician was a waste of time: "She didn't know what I was going through, she just told me the right things to eat!" Kate knew that lack of knowledge about nutrition was the least of her problems.

---

### Box 4.2   Males with Anorexia

Anorexia is often considered a female problem[189] but medical research suggests that 5 to 10 percent of people with anorexia are male[190] and the incidence is highest amongst younger age groups. However, anorexia amongst males may well be under-diagnosed because it is less common than amongst women or because only about half of all males with eating disorders seek treatment.[189] Some research suggests that the incidence of anorexia may be higher amongst men who are more effeminate. However, the reason for this pattern may be because this group is more willing to seek treatment and to admit to a problem that more commonly occurs amongst women.[191]

Males are more likely than females to have been overweight before developing anorexia and to diet in an attempt to be muscular rather than thin.[192] Consequently, anorexia amongst males tends to be more focused on body shape than body weight. Two reasons for weight loss observed amongst males but not amongst females are to compensate for reduced activity following a sporting injury and to avoid the fate of a parent who suffered from a weight-related condition such as heart disease or diabetes.[190,193]

The clinical picture of males and females with anorexia is similar. Both groups tend to avoid foods like carbohydrates and contain a subgroup that uses purging strategies such as vomiting and laxatives. Both groups suffer from higher incidences of other diagnosed mental illnesses than the general population and may struggle in social situations, particularly if they feel uncomfortable about their bodies.[194]

---

Kate was so weak and emaciated that she was admitted to hospital. At the time, she weighed 42 kilos and had a body mass index (BMI) of 15.5. The doctors diagnosed her with anorexia nervosa and decided that her preoccupations with exercising, cleaning, and counting were symptomatic of obsessive-compulsive disorder. Kate was oblivious to the effects of her compulsions or the implications of her severe weight loss. Looking back, Kate admits she was in "total denial." She knew she was "really, really skinny" and felt she "looked disgusting with all my bones sticking out" but also figured "I've gotten this far, why stop now?" Her only priority during her six-week hospitalization was to get out. She believed she was different from all the other girls on the ward. She knew they needed help but was convinced she could recover by herself any time she wanted.

Kate was discharged when she reached her goal weight of 45 kilos. Margie and Carl made sure she attended her regular check-ups and felt she was slowly improving until her doctor suggested it was time to introduce some physiotherapy to "train the muscles up." Margie remembers the moment clearly: "I could see her brain go 'click, click, click—this is exercise' and I thought, 'Oh God.'" As Margie anticipated, Kate's compulsion to exercise returned with a vengeance. Instead of doing one set of each exercise, Kate would do ten. It was horrid for Margie and Carl to watch. Kate would "be hysterical and in a lather of sweat" and her back would be red raw and bruised from doing sit-ups but she "just couldn't stop herself." Margie and Carl put their foot down and banned all exercise, but this just meant that Kate spent hours plotting excuses to exercise: getting Margie to drop her further away from school so she could jog across the sports ground; popping into a neighbor's house; running to the local shops for some inconsequential item. At times Margie and Carl felt they could almost sense the presence of the anorexia:

> It was like it was standing beside her. You could practically see the shadow saying, "Come on. We'll just do a bit more because we don't want to get fat again." You could see it. It was horrible. But she just couldn't stop. She wanted to stop but her brain was just telling her, "Oh come on, let's do a bit more."

Within a few months Kate was readmitted to hospital again. This time around, she had a better idea of what to expect but the highlight of her week remained her physiotherapy session. This was her opportunity to exercise legitimately, albeit under strict supervision, and she'd be agitated and distressed if the physiotherapist was away and she missed an appointment.

Kate hated hospital. She saw the necessity for people who were medically unstable but didn't believe she fitted into that category or that hospital helped prepare you for a life of eating in the outside world:

> We were always being watched and we were always being accused of trying to throw up or exercise in the bathroom. Some girls do that but it's really annoying when you're not doing it. And then you think, "Oh well, maybe I should be." And you've got to go home and you've got to do it for yourself. You can't have nurses feeding you for the rest of your life.

Since Kate's discharge, the family has started a structured family therapy program and meets weekly with their counselor. Margie is delighted. Before family therapy, she and Carl felt as if they were "flying blind," trying to work out how to get around Kate's anorexia without knowing how hard to push or whether they were doing the right thing. What they've learned through family therapy has given them confidence, a structure for day-to-day living, the skills to recognize when the anorexia is "trying to get through," and strategies to stop it controlling their lives.

Margie and Carl work together. At the beginning of each week, they decide on their line of attack so they've got a united approach. Carl comes home from work early so he's around while Margie prepares dinner. That's the most stressful time of the day. It's when Margie's guard is down and when Kate is itching to exercise and getting anxious about eating. It's always around this time that Kate tries to maneuver Margie to give her less dinner or to use lower calorie foods in the menu.

For Margie, the firm approach advocated in family therapy has been a relief. It's completely changed the way the house is organized and run. There's no more individual catering or special meals for Kate and the boys. Margie shops once a week and everyone has to settle for what's in the cupboard. Now the family always sits together at the dining-room table and eats exactly the same meal. Before, the boys were fussy eaters who protested noisily when a meal didn't satisfy their personal fancies. Now they eat whatever is served and they eat a wider range of foods. Margie's also finding they don't get tired or sick as often. Kate is also eating more but this doesn't mean that mealtimes are easy:

There are tantrums because you're giving her just a bit more on her plate, getting her to the table and telling her, "You're going to eat it." [Once you get her to the table] it's not a problem, she eats it. It's just between cooking the food and sitting down to eat it that there's a tantrum... I think it's the fear of how she's going to feel after she's eaten. That's the only way I can explain it. Then she eats dinner and I say, "Well? That wasn't so bad was it?" She says, "No, that was alright." It's really, really strange. It's like there are two different people you're talking to. Like, yesterday wasn't too bad. She said, "What are we having for dinner?" And I said, "We're having spaghetti bolognese." She said, "Well, don't give me a lot." I said, "I'm not giving you a truckload." So we gave her spaghetti bolognese and salad...it was a pretty full plate...there was hardly any tantrum. I don't know how we're going to go tonight because we're having chicken and baked potatoes and vegetables. She likes the chicken that you get in the packs because she's big on this fat free junk and it's really hard to get them off fat free stuff because they count all the calories [laughter]. But I'm just going to buy the chicken and that's it. So I'll just have to see how we go with that!

---

**Box 4.3   Psychiatric Problems Associated with Anorexia**

People with anorexia are more likely than the general population to suffer from other psychiatric problems.[10] Four main *anxiety disorders* are common amongst people with anorexia: generalized anxiety disorder, obsessive-compulsive disorder, panic disorder, and social phobia:

- *Generalized anxiety disorder* causes people to experience excessive anxiety or worry about events or activities in their lives.

- *Obsessive-compulsive disorder* involves persistent, intrusive thoughts or impulses that cause anxiety and distress. Individuals may perform repetitive and excessive actions, such as handwashing, cleaning, or counting.

- *Panic disorder* produces recurring, unexpected panic attacks involving periods of intense fear that cause symptoms such as palpitations, dizziness, feelings of unreality, and fear of dying.

- *Social phobia* involves excessive fear and anxiety triggered by potentially embarrassing social situations that the person will often avoid.[7]

Some studies have found that around half of women with anorexia also suffer from an anxiety disorder at some point in their lives.[10,195] For this group, anxiety is not restricted to weight, eating, and food but relates to other aspects of their lives and causes more widespread distress.

*Depression* is also common amongst people with anorexia. While depression involves feeling sad and hopeless, for some people, especially adolescents and children, it can manifest itself as irritability and might involve regular, angry outbursts over seemingly unimportant incidents.[7] It is estimated that 20 to 80 percent of women with anorexia also suffer from major depression at some time during their lives.[195] Standard treatments for depression and anxiety, such as medication and psychotherapy, are often less effective with underweight individuals than the general community but, in many cases, weight restoration reduces or resolves the symptoms of anxiety and depression.

A range of *personality disorders* have also been associated with anorexia, as well as other eating disorders.[196] A personality disorder is a longstanding pattern of behavior and inner experience that is noticeably different from most other people and that makes it difficult to lead a normal life.[7] The following personality disorders are often associated with anorexia:

- *Avoidant personality disorder* causes people to be very shy, feel inadequate, and be overly sensitive to other people's disapproval.

- *Obsessive-compulsive personality disorder* involves preoccupation with orderliness, perfection, and control.

- *Borderline personality disorder* is characterized by impulsiveness and fluctuating, unstable relationships, self-image, and mood.[7,196,197]

*Autism spectrum disorders* have also been found to be more common in people with anorexia.[198] Typical is Asperger's syndrome, in which people have restricted, repetitive interests and behaviors as well as difficulties with social interactions.

It is not yet known exactly how or why these psychiatric problems are linked to anorexia. They may have a common cause, contribute to the development of anorexia, or be a result of anorexia. However, any additional psychiatric problem complicates the diagnosis and treatment of anorexia.

---

Because of all the hard work put in during the week, Carl is always stressed the night before a family therapy session. This is when Kate will be weighed and Carl's always disappointed when she loses weight and angry if he finds out during therapy that she's been exercising in secret. Family therapy has imposed a new level of openness on all family members. At first, Kate's brothers grizzled and complained about being bored but now they realize the benefits and are beginning to contribute in sessions.

Kate admits family therapy is helping but she doesn't like it. She resents being weighed, resents the time it involves, and hates surrendering control of what she eats to others. But she admits it's made the family closer: "I know when we're over this we'll be a really good family 'cause we look out for each other and 'cause of what we've been through."

Margie and Carl are being firm about other things too. They've banned all exercise, including vacuuming. Carl has even started taking the vacuum cleaner and broom to work in his car. This causes Kate great distress and Margie's patience is waning:

> She'll have the dustpan and brush and be on the ground in hysterics crying, sweeping stuff up off the floor. She does that every now and again when she can't vacuum or sweep and I'm thinking "This is ridiculous, you used to carry on like this when you were two years old."

Being strict is not really in Margie's nature. She feels Carl is a better disciplinarian. "He just bangs the table and says, 'You're eating it. That's it. Don't start.'" Margie and Carl feel Kate's responded well to the firmer approach. She's certainly starting to accept it with better grace. Nevertheless, the constant monitoring and supervision is exhausting and there's little relief in sight. Margie describes it as being "like 24-hour security watch. It's really mentally tiring. It wears you out. It's like you're locked in a cage." Margie feels that "coming down hard" on Kate is necessary to "head off" the anorexia to stop it "coming in the back door" but she knows every slip has consequences:

> It's only going to take one little thing. If you let her get her way with not having margarine on her bread for breakfast—just once—then you can see her head going, "Oh, okay, well we got away with it this time, we'll just try it every other time." You know, "I don't want that. Can I not have this?" You've got to say, "No, you've got to have it. That's it. Over and out." See, if you ease up, it gives the [anorexia] the opportunity to say, "Oh, okay, well we might try and get away with that…" You can see she wants to get better but you can also see that little bit of indecision in the back of her head.

Despite her family's efforts, Kate doesn't believe anyone understands how difficult anorexia *really* is for her:

It's so hard and they don't know how hard it is for me. They think that I like it. I want to get better for them and for me but the anorexia says, "Well, you've got to stay like this for me." It's just comforting knowing you've got it. But they don't tell you that you can get OCD [obsessive-compulsive disorder] or your bones will get thin and you might not be able to play sport for a couple of years 'cause you might break your ankle [and] they don't show how every single second of every single minute of every hour and week is just *so revolved* around it. They've just got *no idea* how *painful* it is mentally and physically. You're going through so much pain if you've got OCD and you're over-exercising [there's] so much stress and pressure [it's] *just horrible*, and scary.

As soon as she gets close to her goal weight, Kate gets scared and cuts back on her eating and starts exercising again. Part of the problem is that Kate feels ambivalent about recovery. Kate feels that one-third of her wants to get better and the remaining two-thirds want to stay the same for the rest of her life. She describes her anorexia as a security blanket. It's been with her for such a long time that it's become inseparable from how she thinks of herself:

You've just got this stereotype of yourself and you just think that if you're not the girl with anorexia, then who are you? You don't know how to be anything else. It's a *part* of me now. It's never fully going to go away from me. It's taken over my life.

At the same time, Kate is frustrated that she can't do all the things she wants to do. She wants to return to a normal life:

We wanted to go skiing this year but I couldn't go 'cause I'd freeze and I'd probably break a bone or something. We just can't be a normal family anymore. 'Cause I love going for runs…my dad promised me that when I get better, he'll come on runs with me and that makes me feel better 'cause it gives me something to aim towards.

For Margie and Carl, this is the sort of admission that gives them hope. Working to help a teenager recover from anorexia, they say, is like chipping away at a granite tomb that encases a precious treasure. It's a matter of slowly chiseling away. Every fragment gets you one step closer to the prize but it's slow work. There's always the threat that the smallest, unintentional slip might damage the treasure beneath.

## Box 4.4   Family Therapy

Family therapy is a type of psychotherapy in which more than one member of the family is included in treatment. It assumes that the family is more than just the sum of its parts and that interactions within the family affect all family members.

Many different types of family therapy are used in treating anorexia. The effectiveness of most models has not been evaluated. Research has been conducted into a model of family-based treatment developed at Maudsley Hospital. This therapy has been found to be effective with adolescents who have had anorexia for less than three years, with 60 to 90 percent of patients recovering.[199] The "Maudsley Approach" involves the therapist educating parents about the physical and psychological effects of anorexia and building an alliance with parents.[200] Parents are encouraged to take charge of their child's eating and the therapist supports them in their efforts to promote weight gain. When the patient's weight and eating have improved, the therapist helps the family give control over eating back to the adolescent. In the last phase of treatment more general issues are explored, such as issues of autonomy and sexuality.

Unlike some forms of family therapy, the "Maudsley Approach" views families as resources for recovery rather than problems that need to be fixed.[129] Other important features of this treatment model are that the therapist has a consultative rather than an authoritarian role and the patient is seen as separate from the anorexia and is not blamed for her or his predicament.[199] While there is evidence that the "Maudsley Approach" to family therapy is effective, it is unclear whether it is the best treatment overall for adolescents because insufficient research has been done on other treatments.[78,94,201]

People diagnosed with anorexia and their families report having different experiences with different types of family therapy. Many have reported that family therapy allowed them to express themselves openly, helped resolve problems in the home, and provided strategies to help them cope.[202] In other situations, family therapy has not been helpful and it can even be a negative experience if people diagnosed with anorexia or their families feel blamed rather than supported.[121]

# 5

# "The Problem Isn't You, It's the Anorexia"
## The Story of Hannah, Laura, Peter, and Luke

In the still air of the evening, the historic family home is wrapped in the scent of camphor from the large old trees that line the long driveway. The house is filled with antiques and the paraphernalia of an energetic, athletic family—assorted sporting equipment and the trophies and ribbons accumulated over the years by Laura and Peter and their two children, Hannah and Luke. The large old house looks very much like it did a hundred years ago. The only major change is that Laura and Peter have installed huge wardrobes in the oversized bedrooms.

At first glance Hannah seems like a girl who has it all—a lovely home, a close family, and popularity with her peers. She excels at school and her wiry, muscular frame has made her a promising competitive swimmer. With the help of coaching from Peter, Hannah was only 13 years old when she won a place in the state swimming squad. Hours of intense swimming training each day guaranteed that Hannah was constantly hungry. She'd often stop in at her mother's café for a muffin and milkshake to and from school and she could always be relied on to eat whatever was served for dinner and then to ask for seconds.

When Hannah made the swimming squad, her driving goal was to beat her main rival in the team. It was when she was at an intensive training camp that Hannah came across an idea that might give her the competitive edge she craved:

> The swimming season was coming up. I wanted to do really well and I really wanted to beat this girl. I read a book that said the best body fat percentage for competitive swimmers was 17 percent. So I got my body

fat checked at the gym and it was 23 percent. So I decided I wanted to lower my body fat. I didn't have any specific issues about weight. I didn't even know how much I weighed. That never bothered me because I was always muscled. According to all the tables, I was already overweight because muscle weighs more than fat. That didn't worry me and I didn't feel fat. I just wanted to decrease my body fat a little bit so I could beat her. And I lost weight healthily for about a year just by decreasing the junk food and chocolate—I was a real chocoholic—and by doing a little bit more exercise. But not super-duper amounts.

Hannah took up jogging on top of her regular swimming training and gym workouts. Since her only goal was to get fit and healthy there didn't seem to be any obvious cause for concern. In fact, Peter remembers how much like the average teenager Hannah seemed:

She was eating a lot of salads but she'd cut out fat completely and she was playing with being a vegetarian. She was reading lots of diet books but we figured she was just experimenting with her food. I've always thought that teenage girls tend to get a lot of their information from things like *Dolly* magazines and *Girlfriend* magazines and I just put it down as one of those stages she was going through because things kept changing—you know, this week it was vegetarian, next week it was protein, next week it is carbohydrate. It was just play time. She certainly wasn't ill or sick in any way. She was really healthy and swimming well, and she strutted around the beach looking at all the 16-year-old boys and they were checking her out as well and that was really good.

The first obvious sign that Hannah's dieting was entangled with something more than a desire to be healthy came just before she was due to go away to camp with her school. She was anxious and agitated. What sort of food would they have at camp? What if they didn't have the food she wanted? How would she manage? How could she stick to her current diet? The idea of varying what she ate, even for two weeks, sent her into a spin. The food at camp didn't help. It was the usual school camp fare—lots of bread, pastries, and oily, fried dinners. Confronted with this menu, Hannah either refused to eat or ate the bare minimum and ran 15 kilometers each day to offset what she'd eaten. Her teachers were so concerned that they contacted Laura and Peter:

> Apparently what had happened at camp was that if they didn't have what she wanted she just wouldn't eat. She'd just have a plate of peas for dinner if there was nothing else on the menu she'd accept. (Laura)

When Peter collected Hannah from camp, her face was sunken and grey, her T-shirt hung on her like an oversized sack and her arms and legs were so thin that they looked as if they might shatter. But it was Hannah's conversation during the long car trip home that convinced Peter that they were dealing with more than a diet gone wrong:

> I'll be honest, I didn't recognize her. She'd lost so much weight in the weeks she was away. She just looked awful. And all she talked about in the car on the way home was where she ate, what she ate. Meal by meal. In the hour and a half trip home, I don't think she told me anything about their lessons or what they saw. It was "We went to a place, we had a meal there, and this is what I had." So she knew it meal by meal. When we got home and I had a chance to talk to Laura I said, "We've got a problem here." It scared me. It worried us.

They weren't the only ones who were scared. Hannah was also worried. What concerned her, Peter remembers, was her fading energy: "Hannah knew she had a problem too because the first thing she said when we hopped in the car was, 'I have to go to a doctor.' She was worried about iron deficiency...about her iron count being low because she was so tired."

Laura and Peter insisted the dieting and jogging stop. They took Hannah to a series of doctors but each time she found an excuse to avoid seeing that doctor again and to buy a little more time: she wouldn't go to a local doctor; she didn't want a male doctor; she didn't like a particular doctor. Despite Hannah's resistance, Peter felt her exercise and anxieties about food seemed to ease:

> For a while there she fought it and she seemed to pick up a bit. Laura was monitoring what she was eating and I was monitoring her exercise because I was doing swimming training with her. As weak as she looked, I figured she must be okay if she could still do her swimming and running. I guess in my mind there was still some denial.

The respite was short lived. Bit by bit, Hannah reduced the range of foods she'd eat. There was no particular rationale. She just couldn't face eating food:

She'd pick up food and say, "I can't eat that." Or "I'd love to eat that but I can't." And I'd say, "Well, why can't you?" "Oh, because I can't." And I'd say, "Well, you know, just have a mouthful. Just have a bite and see what you think." It was like everything else is out of control but she could keep an exactness with her food. It was the only thing that she could. She knew it was going to be the same every day. And the more that happened outside, the more she tightened up on the food. (Laura)

Laura and Peter begged her to eat something different—just a little meat, bread, or pasta—but their pleas were ignored. Eventually, Hannah was surviving on little more than carrots and her skin turned orange from the betacarotene. At the same time, she became increasingly suspicious. She insisted on weighing everything before she ate it and would carefully monitor its calories. The family had always eaten healthy, home-cooked meals together but, increasingly, Hannah refused to eat anything prepared by someone else. In Laura's words, "She wouldn't trust any of my cooking." Though Hannah had never liked soft drink, she started consuming liters of low-calorie fizzy drink at every meal but no one was allowed to touch her bottles of soft drink. She was afraid they would spike it with supplements. Hannah also started keeping a food diary:

> Part of her downfall was the fact that she wrote everything down. She would leave the table halfway through the meal and start writing into the food diary. But she was very particular in what she wrote down. I mean down to the calorie. She was weighing *everything* and writing it down. (Peter)

Eventually, Hannah insisted on preparing all her own food. This drove Laura to distraction:

> At mealtimes, she'd eat exact things at exactly the same time and there were all these little rituals. She'd get a carrot out of the fridge. She'd peel it. She'd top and tail it, she'd slice it. She'd lay it out in the steamer. She'd cook it for one and a half minutes. She'd get it out and she'd eat. And then she'd go to the fridge and she'd get another carrot out. And she'd top and tail it. And then she'd weigh it before it was cooked and she'd weigh it after it was cooked. Then she'd go on to the frozen vegetables. She'd get a packet of frozen vegetables or a frozen dinner out and read the nutritional value on the back and write it down. Then she would pour it out of the bag and weigh it, then heat it in the microwave, then take it out, weigh it,

reheat it again, then weigh it and eat it. It was the same order with every single meal, every single day.

When she'd sit with the vegetables, she'd turn the plate and she'd have three mouthfuls. Then she'd turn the plate and eat three mouthfuls and so on. I'd say to her, "If you're going to eat two bags of vegetables every night, get the big steamer out and cook the whole lot and then sit down and eat with us." But she couldn't because it was too daunting, that much food. She'd have to serve it up in these little portions... It nearly drove us bonkers, it really did. It would take her anything up to two and a half hours to eat dinner each night but her total calories was probably only 200 calories. It was mind-blowingly annoying. She knew she was doing it but she couldn't help it. If there was any friction at the meal table she was worse. And if we hadn't bought things, we'd have to go shopping and have the exact products in the right part of the fridge or she'd throw a hysterical screaming fit. It was really frustrating.

---

### Box 5.1 Effects of Starvation

The behaviors of people with anorexia can be frustrating for families and friends, and are often considered to be "abnormal" and indicative of mental illness. However, some of the behaviors of people with anorexia can be a consequence of starvation. Research shows that even healthy people exhibit anorexic behaviors when they deliberately starve themselves of food. Three examples illustrate the connection between starvation and behavior:

1. During World War II, a group of 36 healthy conscientious objectors of normal weight participated in an experiment to study the effects of starvation and refeeding. The aim of the research was to help plan rehabilitation programs for starving people from occupied countries. The men had to restrict their eating severely for six months to lose a quarter of their body weight.[203]

2. During the early 1990s, eight scientists and technicians involved in a self-sustained living experiment found that they were unable to produce as much food as they expected. Rather than drop out of the experiment they spent two years on rations that provided enough nutrients but were very low on calories.[204] The four men and four women lost an average of 20 percent and 13 percent of their body weights respectively.

3. People who practice caloric restriction for longevity (CRL) reduce their food intake by up to 40 percent in the hope of staving off the aging process and living longer.[205] CRL was inspired by the results of laboratory experiments in which animals were fed nutrient-dense diets that contained very few calories. The underfed animals lived longer and aged more slowly than animals on a normal diet, apparently due to a complex biological shift from a growth and reproduction mode to a life maintenance mode.[206]

In each of these groups people have shown many classic anorexic symptoms and behaviors such as depression, irritability, obsessionality, apathy and lack of initiative, social withdrawal, and sexual disinterest. They became highly preoccupied with food, collected recipes and pictures of food, fantasized about food, and hoarded and stole food. They spent inordinate amounts of time eating their meager rations and some developed odd eating rituals or sporadically broke down and binged. Many found it difficult to return to normal eating afterward and reported binge eating, food obsession, and feelings of lack of control about eating.[207–9]

Like other animals, human beings have complex defenses against food restriction and these keep people unhappy and preoccupied with food until they are fed adequately.[210] Many clinicians believe that, below a particular weight threshold, people with anorexia are unable to really benefit from psychological therapies.[155] While weight restoration alone is not a "cure" for anorexia, recognizing that the behavior of people with anorexia is similar to the normal reaction of individuals to starvation can make anorexia a little more comprehensible for families, friends, and those diagnosed with anorexia.

Formerly placid and relaxed, Hannah's newly developed passion for precision extended into other areas of her daily life. She'd fly into a rage at the slightest irritation, "like if my clothes weren't washed on time or I had a wrinkle in my skirt." More often than not, these episodes degenerated into "yelling, screaming, slanging matches" that reduced Hannah and her mother to tears.

Hannah's friends noticed the change in her behavior. She was always tired at school and often fell asleep during class. She was "snappy and snarly" and began making excuses not to go out with her friends or to talk to them when they phoned. Eventually, her friends gave up on her. Peter would take Hannah with him when he went swimming, but instead of hanging around, giggling with her girlfriends and flirting with the boys, Hannah now sat alone in the clubhouse swathed in layers of clothing.

Laura and Peter found themselves "walking on eggshells" to avoid unwittingly doing or saying something that would cause an explosion. They also worried about Luke. Hannah had always been his strong, big sister and he missed the hours they spent chatting in the huge bedroom wardrobe in his room. Instead, Hannah was always upset and cranky and would "snap his head off" without provocation. Luke was so shattered by the transformation that he withdrew into his own private world:

> Luke didn't speak for about three months really. He just clammed right up. It was very hard for him. His sister had always been his knight in shining armor, I suppose. She'd always been this invincible person who could do absolutely anything. Everything she did was perfect and he just loved her to death. And to see her like this. He would say [whispering], "Why doesn't she eat? Why doesn't she eat? She's going to die." But he couldn't do anything about it. He was lost. He withdrew and stopped speaking. He wasn't naughty. He just didn't speak. The school contacted me because they were so very concerned about his behavior. As she got better, he got better. (Laura)

By now, Hannah's weight had dropped to 41 kilos and she only had 11 percent body fat. Her circulation was poor and she had little energy. She couldn't do her swimming training anymore and could only manage two to three hours of school each day. Nevertheless, Hannah couldn't see that the anorexia had overtaken her. To their relief, Laura and Peter eventually found a doctor who wouldn't let Hannah off the hook. Laura remembers that every consultation was preceded by Hannah "cursing and swearing like a woman possessed" but the doctor just ignored the resistance and complaints:

> She was fairly brash, fairly hard, and fairly straight down the line. She didn't mince words with Hannah [and told her] "You will hate me. You will despise me… I don't care. I'm your doctor and I'm going to get you better." She knew Hannah could manipulate us but she couldn't manipulate her. She played hard ball and wouldn't let Hannah get away with anything. She'd make her sit in the surgery for an hour—sometimes it was twice a week—and wouldn't let Hannah out the door. Hannah would get really cranky but the doctor would say, "Sit down. I haven't finished speaking to you yet." Sometimes we were invited in and

sometimes we weren't. Hannah would get up and go and get a magazine and start reading it and the doctor would say, "Put the magazine down and come back here. I'm speaking to you." I think she was a real turning point. Hannah knew that once or twice a week she had to see her and there was going to be no mincing of words.

Despite lacking the energy, Hannah was adamant that she couldn't survive without exercising. For Laura and Peter, the question of how to handle this compulsion was a major dilemma. Given Hannah's history as an elite athlete, they thought banning all exercise would damage Hannah's psychological stability and her doctor agreed. However, any exercise was limited to sessions at the gym that were strictly supervised by Laura. The plan fell apart when other gym members complained to the manager about Hannah. They insisted that Hannah looked so thin and sick that she shouldn't be allowed to exercise. Confronted with such opposition, the manager withdrew Hannah's gym membership. Laura was angry and upset that people didn't talk to her before complaining. If they'd done so, Laura would have explained what a delicate emotional juggling act they were trying to perform with Hannah. Hannah's response was more serious. She embarked on a secret exercise program. She'd wake at 3 am each morning and run 12 kilometers before returning to bed. Her weight plummeted and Hannah's doctors and parents were mystified.

In hindsight, Peter suspects that Hannah wanted them to discover her secret because she left her jogging shoes and clothes lying under the window. He feels foolish that it took two months to figure it out, but he had trouble believing that Hannah was capable of deception. After they woke one night and discovered Hannah's bed empty, Laura and Peter confronted her. Peter remembers that "The look on her face was almost like relief…she'd had this secret there for so long and she felt guilty about hiding it from us but she wasn't able to tell us."

Now Laura and Peter were worried about what Hannah might do if they left her alone. Already juggling busy work schedules and looking after the needs of both children, they now had to develop elaborate strategies so that Hannah was always supervised. Peter believes that anorexia works on the principle of "divide and conquer" and Hannah went through phases of refusing to talk with one or other parent. Laura and Peter managed by working together as a team:

Peter would spend time with Hannah and then when he was ready to strangle her, we would swap. Luke and I went to the pictures a lot. We went out to tea a lot. We'd spend a lot of time going for drives just to get away. And then we'd come home and Peter would go out so that he could have time out to regroup.

---

**Box 5.2   Influence of Siblings**

Siblings and sibling relationships have a powerful influence on adolescents, including their experiences of anorexia and recovery.[211-13] Our research shows that there are three main ways in which well siblings influence a person diagnosed with anorexia.[214]

1.  Siblings exert an influence simply by their presence in the family and the home.

    - They can unknowingly cause problems just by going about their normal activities if, for example, these disturb the routines of the person with anorexia.

    - Some people diagnosed with anorexia contend that actions by a sibling, such as going on a crash diet, may have contributed to their anorexia.

    - Individuals diagnosed with anorexia may compare their lives and achievements in personal, academic, or sporting arenas to those of their siblings.

    - Individuals diagnosed with anorexia may feel anxious and guilty about the possibility that their anorexia could have a negative effect on a sibling.

2.  Siblings exercise influence through their responses to the person with anorexia and the way these are interpreted.

    - Some people diagnosed with anorexia feel their siblings reject or avoid them because of the anorexia.

    - Some people diagnosed with anorexia see siblings as uninvolved in or oblivious to their anorexia and view sibling relationships as unchanged. This can mean the loss of a potential source of support but can also mean that a normal sibling relationship can be maintained at a difficult time.

---

- Many siblings try to help and support the individual with anorexia. They provide practical help such as bringing work home from school. They visit and spend time in hospital, provide comfort, and show love and affection. They try to avoid upsetting and they forgive the behavior of the person diagnosed with anorexia. Older siblings may confront their siblings about the anorexia, express their concerns and give advice, information, and encouragement.

3. Siblings influence parents and parents' ability to cope and this has an indirect influence on the person with anorexia.

- Parents have to divide their time and attention between siblings. This can mean finding compromises to meet the needs of siblings and the child with anorexia.[214]

- Parents can become more stressed and anxious if the anorexia has a negative impact on siblings.

- Having other children who are well can be comforting and redress parents' concerns that their parenting may have somehow caused the anorexia.

- Siblings support their parents by supporting the child with anorexia.

- Siblings may offer their parents helpful opinions, information, and advice.

- Siblings may act as go-betweens or buffers between parents and the child with anorexia when relationships are strained and difficult.

The nature and extent of siblings' influence is affected by different factors including how much the sibling understands about anorexia, how much parents and the individual diagnosed with anorexia encourage or discourage siblings' involvement in the anorexia, the kind of relationship siblings in the family had before the anorexia, and the life the well sibling leads. Factors like the ages and gender of siblings, their personalities and backgrounds, the number of siblings in the family, and the duration of the anorexia can also have an impact, but these appear to occur mainly via the factors listed above. While factors like age and gender of siblings are fixed, factors like sibling understanding can be influenced by the efforts of parents and health professionals.[215,216] However, the well-being of siblings is an important consideration and very little is currently known about how they are affected by being encouraged or expected to support a sibling with anorexia.

While Laura dragged an unwilling Hannah to the doctor, Peter trawled the internet and read a seemingly endless stream of information about anorexia. One idea slowly captured his imagination, a notion used in narrative therapy treatments for anorexia. The idea is that the anorexia is separate from the person with anorexia, almost like a different, distinct individual. Laura and Luke were attracted by the idea that Hannah was the victim of a stronger, separate entity. It helped them see that they were struggling and fighting the anorexia, not their daughter and sister. For Peter, the idea of personifying the anorexia was a major breakthrough:

> We said, "Hannah, we love you. We'll always love you but this person that's in you—this possessed person that's in you—we hate her. We want her gone." So we actually talked about Hannah and the other person. And when we made the definition and she made the definition, it was a lot easier to deal with.

Luke christened Hannah's anorexia "The Bitch." Now he could relate to his sister and he'd cuddle and console Hannah, reassuring her that "The problem isn't you, it's the anorexia."

Initially, Hannah was dubious about the idea of personifying her anorexia. Yet somehow the notion gave her a new set of emotional resources and "suddenly I could just see the anorexia wasn't me and that there was a way to get better."

When she next saw her doctor, however, Hannah learned that her liver count was seriously high and that she needed to be hospitalized. Having just turned 16 years of age and having finally found a possible entry point for recovering, the need to be hospitalized triggered a complex response:

> She came home and she turned into a two-year-old. She got all these dolls out and she started playing with all these dolls. Her brain had just snapped. She started playing with these dolls and jumping around and skipping and she was throwing all these dolls. I said, "What's wrong?" [she said] "I'm free." It was almost as if the doctor saying she had to go to hospital was a relief. She didn't have to control anything anymore because they were going to take control. And then she went *really* quiet and locked herself in her room for about three hours. She was just sitting there just not doing anything—like she was in shock. The doctor said, "She's reverted to her childhood because she's been so traumatized by the fact that the control is going to be taken away from her"... Then about five o'clock in the afternoon she started. There was this temper—a

screaming, slanging match. And throwing furniture, throwing anything she could. Screaming, punching, yelling. Just this hysterical sobbing… I was just completely blown away. (Laura)

---

## Box 5.3   Support Networks for Parents and Carers

Parents and carers often need practical and emotional support as well as information and advice to cope with the demands of anorexia.[217] Health professionals are an important source of support but other types of support are also available.

### Support groups

Many eating disorder associations sponsor support groups and these are listed on their websites. Such groups aim to help parents and carers understand and look after their children, provide education about anorexia and treatments, share coping and management strategies, and offer information about how carers can support themselves, their partners, and other children. Some eating disorder associations offer telephone or email counseling so carers can get one-to-one support.

Other support groups are run by medical and health professionals, by parents of people who have recovered from anorexia, or by parents and clinicians working together. For example, the Flemish association Vereniging Anorexia Nervosa and Boulima Nervosa (VANBN) organised a Parents for Parents support group. Health professionals trained volunteer parents with recovered children who then organized discussion groups for carers and visited schools to talk about eating disorders.[218]

### Online support

A number of carer support sites are available on the internet. Many are based in the USA but are linked to similar sites in the UK, Germany, Israel, Mexico, Australia, and elsewhere. Support sites provide information about eating disorders, treatment, and research as well as online support groups and chat rooms where carers can share experiences and knowledge.

### Informal support

Many parents and carers establish informal support networks with relatives, friends, and work colleagues, or through church and community groups. Others find support from other parents and carers whom they

---

have met at hospitals and treatment centers. Such networks offer flexibility and different levels and forms of support.

### Strengths and weaknesses of support groups.

Not everyone has equal access to support groups. For instance, people in smaller towns or rural areas may not be close to a support group. Access to the necessary technology for online support may not be available. The positive benefits of a support group include sharing experiences and knowledge and developing new insights. A support group can reduce the sense of being alone and help carers clarify their thoughts and feelings and receive acknowledgement and care for the difficulties they experience.[146] A structured, formal support group may not suit everyone's needs. Some parents report feeling uncomfortable and reluctant to share their problems or to hear about the difficulties of others and witness their distress. Ideally, parents and carers should draw on a range of networks that are best suited to their needs.

The day Hannah was to be admitted to hospital was also the day of the school swimming carnival. In the past, she'd always won every race. This year she couldn't even compete. Hannah hugged Luke as he left for the carnival saying, "The Bitch has just taken two years of my life and she's not going to take one more second." Before they left for the hospital, Hannah insisted on a large breakfast and tried a piece of chocolate to see if the anorexia would "psyche" her out. The experiment was a success and Laura and Peter had to stop five times to buy food on the way to the hospital. By the time they arrived, Hannah was nearly two kilos heavier than when she'd been weighed by her doctor the day before.

Peter and Laura weren't sure about the sincerity of Hannah's transformation. Peter suspected it was just a ploy to get out of hospital because he felt, "There's a lot of lying involved in being anorexic." As time went on, however, it was obvious Hannah was determined to get better. She'd already proved she could be "the best dieter." Now she set out to prove that she could be the best at getting better.

Recovery, however, is rarely straightforward, but whenever Hannah felt discouraged she'd phone her father. Their chats always made her feel better. When Peter and Luke visited, they told Hannah that anorexia cowered in a corner of her bedroom but it was getting smaller and smaller because they'd beat it up each night. Laura and Peter also encouraged Hannah's friends to visit and phone her and Hannah found that much of her time in hospital was spent rebuilding fractured relationships by explaining that it was the anorexia—not her—that had slighted her friends.

Hannah was discharged after three weeks—a week earlier than her doctors had predicted—weighing 50 kilos. Despite the positive progress, Laura and Peter were apprehensive that her old behaviors would resurface when she came home. The family agreed it would be better if anorexia wasn't waiting for Hannah when she came home so Peter and Luke hatched a plot: "We told Hannah that we'd been a bit heavy handed and we'd wiped [The Bitch] out completely."

Four months later, Hannah's recovery is continuing. She's still very disciplined about what she eats but she now aims to eat 2500 rather than 600 calories a day. Her liver function isn't back to normal and she hasn't started menstruating again but her doctors expect these problems to right themselves eventually.

Throughout Hannah's illness, Laura and Peter have appreciated the support from Hannah and Luke's school. Hannah's teachers always made themselves available to talk, even outside of school hours, and this reassured Peter and Laura that they weren't the only ones looking after Hannah. At one stage, one of Hannah's teachers phoned Laura almost daily to keep her up to date on Hannah's progress. When Hannah finally returned to school, the principal made a point of welcoming her back and expressing delight that she'd returned and was looking so well. Laura also found support from an informal network of women friends, ranging in age from 18 to 50 years. They provided a sympathetic ear and valuable practical support by picking up Laura's load whenever she had to take time off work. They also shared their stories of similar experiences with their own daughters and with the daughters of their friends. Knowing how others survived helped Laura during the tough times.

Hannah's thinking about going back to swimming training but dismisses the idea of competitive swimming. She's lost so much time with anorexia it would be a struggle to regain her form and she doesn't want to risk returning to the culture of competitive swimming and falling into the same trap that she fell into years ago. Instead, Hannah is focusing on the

## Box 5.4   Advice from Parents and Carers

Parents and carers often have difficulty working out how to help someone diagnosed with anorexia and how to cope with their own personal challenges and distress. Because every person's circumstances are different there are no foolproof solutions or guaranteed answers, but parents have shared the following advice.[219]

### Things to do

- Parents may receive conflicting advice. It is important for parents and carers not to uncritically accept or reject everything they're told but to educate themselves so that they have the knowledge to make informed decisions.
- Keep the lines of communication open and constantly remind the person with anorexia that they are supported and loved.
- Be proactive about finding the right treatment program and, when this is found, work closely with the clinicians so the person diagnosed with anorexia gets consistent messages from everyone.
- It is important to keep sight of and attend to the needs of other family members.
- Parents and carers need to look after their own physical and mental well-being for their own sake and the sake of their families.

### Ways of thinking

- An optimistic outlook is important.
- It can be helpful to think of the anorexia as separate from the person with anorexia because this allows parents to loathe the anorexia but love their child.
- Parents and carers should not blame themselves or the person with anorexia for the illness.
- Parents and carers need to accept their limitations and recognize that they cannot *make* someone diagnosed with anorexia recover or be perfect *all* the time and in *every* situation.
- Parents and carers often hope a family will eventually be the same as before the anorexia. This may be unrealistic and it can be better to move forward and to establish a different but still positive relationship.

future. She wants to be a dietician when she leaves school. She believes her own suffering and difficulties with food will enable her to help young girls who also have similar traumas.

Laura and Peter believe the most positive step they made in helping Hannah's recovery was by doing their own research and learning to differentiate Hannah from her anorexia. For their family, this was a key breakthrough. At the same time, they've survived on pure adrenalin, very little sleep and suffered "absolute burnout" but, compared to other parents, they believe they've been lucky. Hannah's illness only lasted three years. They empathize with parents whose daughters have been sick for many years.

# 6

# "Tough Love"
## The Story of Jo, Julie, Michael, and Sam

The house looks like all the others in the comfortable beach-side suburb but inside it's scarred by years of Jo's rages: the furniture is battered; the ornaments and paintings are gone; the doors are dented, scratched, or missing; and the windows have been broken and fixed more often than anyone can remember. Julie and Michael still carry a hint of an accent in their voices even though they migrated from England more than 20 years ago. Their children, 18-year-old Josephine and 15-year-old Sam, are the center of their parents' world and they both inherited Julie's typically English looks: blonde hair, blue eyes, and a complexion with the translucence of bone china.

As a child, Josephine's curly blonde hair and sweet, engaging nature won the hearts of everyone. Before long, it was obvious that the nickname "Jo" was a more accurate reflection of her personality than the more formal Josephine. Like her girlfriends, Jo was a tomboy—more interested in swimming and surfing than boys or fashion. Julie and Michael remember those years fondly. That was a time when Jo seemed like every other teenager they knew. Today, Jo is still classically pretty—almost angelic—but the placid persona she presents to the world disguises a turbulent, tortured soul.

Ever since she was a toddler, Jo always had odd eating patterns and was willful about food. She wouldn't allow any two foods on her plate to touch—not even pasta with tomato sauce—and always ate her food in a fixed, non-negotiable order: meat, salad, and then potato followed by other vegetables. Jo stuck to this inflexible ritual everywhere and without fail. When she was 15 years old, Jo announced that she'd decided to become a vegetarian. Michael and Julie decided not to fuss:

I know all kids go through the vegetarian phase. So if Jo didn't want to eat meat, I didn't have a problem. We just bought extra vegetables and rice. I didn't want to make an issue about it. If you make an issue out of it then it will become a problem. And she never loved meat particularly anyway. (Julie)

There were bigger changes when Jo got her first boyfriend. A boyfriend was a status symbol at Jo's elite private girls' school—a public statement that you were popular, desirable, mature, and a "real" woman. Her circle of friends widened and there were new social opportunities. Jo quietly relished her newfound persona until a silly, spiteful quip sent her spinning:

I was happy. I was healthy. I ate what I wanted. I exercised. I was sporty. Then, a stupid boy called me fat. It was really pathetic but at that age when someone says something, you believe it and take it to heart—especially girls. Call a boy fat and he'd forget about it the next day. Call a girl fat and they're not going to forget it—even though the boy who said it can't even remember saying it. I got called fat at a time when you start to get conscious of your weight, around 15 or 16 years of age. To get called fat was a big blow. I took it really seriously and wanted to lose that weight and to get healthy and fit. I started trying to get healthy but it got muddled up. I guess I was one of those people who took it one step too far.

It was a blatantly unkind and untrue remark but it rocked Jo. Behind the bravado of being grown-up was a fragile, insecure teenager:

That was the real catalyst—the real beginning. Boys can be very cruel…she was with her boyfriend and one of his friends turned around and said that she wasn't good enough for him and she was fat and ugly. (Michael)

Yeah, that's what happened. That's what they're like at that age, it's horrible. Another person would probably get angry and tell them where to go, but she unfortunately had always been sensitive and taken things to heart. That's her personality. (Julie)

The culture at Jo's school didn't help. In the disciplined, competitive environment, being slender was a highly desired attribute. It marked girls out as self-disciplined, high achievers—the sorts of people who were destined to succeed in all walks of life—and those who didn't fit the approved mold found themselves alienated, excluded, and alone. Girls competed to lose weight but they also shared diets, weight-loss tricks, and laxatives. One of

Jo's friends even wrote her detailed instructions on how to make herself vomit after eating. Michael and Julie couldn't control the culture at Jo's school but Julie formed the view that "they all seem to have eating disorders."

---

## Box 6.1 School Culture and Anorexia

Schools play a major part in the lives of children and teenagers. Schools are places where young people not only acquire academic knowledge but also learn about social and cultural rules, relationships, and expectations. They are important sites for the development of students' self-image and confidence. Schools venerate and encourage three particular "virtue discourses" (i.e. values and ways of thinking) that can unwittingly feed into the attitudes and behaviors evident amongst teenagers with anorexia.[163]

### The virtue of self-discipline

Schools are highly structured, disciplined environments. Bells, timetables, and rules regulate the use of time: lessons and mealtimes are fixed; the curriculum is taught in designated timeframes; assignments and assessment tasks have schedules and deadlines; and exam times are carefully controlled and monitored. Explicit and implicit rules dictate where it is permissible to be physically located (e.g. the classroom, playground, library, gymnasium) and the acceptable activities in these spaces (e.g. silence/talking, work/play, games/learning, eating/not eating). The disciplinary mechanisms of schools present self-discipline as a virtue and as the demonstration of a disciplined, controlled life.[163]

The virtue of self-discipline that is highly regarded in schools can echo and reinforce anorexic behaviors and values. This is evident, for instance, when teenagers with anorexia segment their lives into tidy timeslots with specific purposes and impose tightly disciplined routines on their eating and exercise routines.

### The virtue of individual achievement

Competition and achievement are highly valued in schools and many students feel pressured to compete with their peers and to be successful, high achievers.[183,220] Schools encourage competition through assessments and exam practices, sporting activities, and competitive entry to privileged activities, for example, a school band or a sports team. Schools publicly award winners and high achievers with prizes, privileges, and

---

prestige. In contrast, non-achievement is an undesirable and unwanted state that signifies failure.[163]

Where competition and individual achievement are highly prized values, some teenagers extend these values to their own bodies. Food abstinence (self-starvation) can be viewed as an area of personal expertise and achievement, and as a sort of success. In contrast, non-achievement is equated with failure and is evident in the comments of weight-recovered anorexics who describe themselves as failed anorexics.[74]

## The virtue of being healthy *and* thin

The importance of being thin is promoted in schools through its link to health in the physical education and health curriculum.[221] Schools also make students' bodies objects of public display in ways that nurture physical comparisons, for instance, through institutionalized dress codes and at events such as swimming and athletics carnivals, school dances, sport and gym classes. The regulation of mealtimes at school normalizes eating behaviors by making food consumption a public act amenable to moral surveillance by peers and others, and where lack of self-discipline about the type or quantity of food eaten is susceptible to commentary or ridicule by peers.

When students are encouraged to be slender and healthy by dieting and exercising, it can nurture the idea of bodies as problems to be controlled and as objects for self-discipline and achievement.[70] There may be even greater pressure for students to be thin if they aspire to be a higher achiever in areas such as sport or ballet.[183,222]

Students' experiences of school are also shaped in informal settings such as the playground, friendship groups, and social situations through school and extracurricular activities. When peer groups place a priority on losing weight, or being thin, it can contribute to a culture of disordered eating and researchers have identified this phenomenon in some colleges in the United States.[223] These sorts of experiences are of concern to schools. Schools do not consciously set out to contribute to eating disorders, but the education policies and school practices that endorse and exaggerate the virtues of discipline, competition, and being healthy and thin can result in pressures and conditions that may be detrimental to the health of young people. For these reasons, recovering from anorexia may mean going against the virtues that are fostered as part of the daily routine, social practices, and policy frameworks under which schools operate.

Determined never to be labeled "fat" again, Jo gradually started dieting and exercising but this soon degenerated into hours of jogging and swimming each day. It was an unsustainable regime for a starving body and by the evening Jo was so hungry that she'd binge on whatever she could lay her hands on: cakes, vegetables, junk food, pasta, anything. Afterwards, she was always distraught and full of remorse and self-loathing. She'd do anything necessary to purge herself of what she'd eaten.

Julie and Michael worried about Jo's weight loss. When Julie caught her vomiting after a night out, she thought the cause was too much alcohol rather than anorexic behaviors. In Jo's new social circle, weekends consisted of a string of parties and alcohol was freely available. For Jo, alcohol was a way "to get away from it all from me, my mind, my thinking." Julie and Michael loathed the weekends:

> All the kids seem to go out and binge drink and get blind drunk. We dreaded—absolutely dreaded—Friday and Saturday nights because we'd get phone calls from her boyfriend or her friends to come and pick her up. I'd either have to pick her up from the gutter because she was incapable of walking or she'd jump out of the car and run away because she was so drunk. She kept saying, "I'm 16 and you can't tell me what to do." (Michael)

Michael and Julie felt trapped and powerless. They didn't want to stop Jo from going to the parties that were just a regular part of growing up as a teenager, but they couldn't do anything to stop the damage she inflicted on herself when she went out. They talked about the different options and ways forward for hours on end. At each turn, their choices were constrained by the same dilemma every parent faces: how to protect your child from harm but allow them the freedom to learn about life?

Events came to a head as the date of Jo's debutante ball inched closer. This was to be an extravagant, formal event and the highlight of the year's social calendar. For months, Jo and her girlfriends had been talking about the gowns they'd wear, the boys who would escort them, the "before" and "after" parties, and the elaborate pomp and ceremony of this old-fashioned presentation to society. Unbeknown to Michael and Julie, for months Jo had been starving herself and vomiting and abusing laxatives in an effort to be thin and svelte for the ball. She'd lost so much weight that her dress swam on her but she doggedly insisted that she was too fat to be seen in public and refused to go to the ball.

This episode galvanized Michael and Julie and they finally vocalized what they'd both silently suspected for a long time: Jo's behavior was symptomatic of more serious issues. Julie organized for Jo to avoid the ball by taking her to visit friends out of town but not before they located a pediatrician who specialized in adolescent eating disorders. Jo took an immediate liking to him. He prescribed antidepressants and a second visit was organized for when they returned.

Julie and Michael hoped that a break would stabilize Jo and that their family life would return to normal. Jo did seem more settled and contented when she came home and she saw her specialist periodically—until a friend's little sister passed a flippant comment about Jo's "flabby" thighs. Jo was devastated. As soon as she got home, Jo turned on herself in a violent rage, trashing her bedroom, emptying the cupboards onto the floor, and smashing ornaments and pictures. She hacked off her cherished long blonde hair and slashed her thighs with a knife so severely that the scars still remain. Finally she swallowed an entire packet of herbal sedatives in a forlorn search for peace.

This episode shocked and frightened the whole family. They hoped it was an isolated incident but it was the beginning of a downhill spiral of self-destruction. As Julie explains, a clear pattern quickly emerged:

> She'd starve for days. Then eat and binge and binge. Then she'd starve. Her normal pattern is she won't eat all day—or she might have juice or a banana—then she'll eat in the evening and vomit in the night and then stop and not eat for ages. That's why the doctors called it anorexic bulimic.

Jo's black rages were often the effect of the self-loathing that invariably followed a binge. At other times they were triggered by a flippant passing comment or simply by the stress of trying to get through life:

> Sometimes I lose it because I'd been putting on this act of trying to be happy and eating and doing all that. It would really just take its toll on me and I'd lose it every now and then. I'd get the shits. I've smashed up the kitchen, thrown ketchup bottles and things all over the kitchen. Just destroyed it. Afterwards, I feel like a monster and an animal.

Remembering these incidents, Michael and Julie paint a picture of a sort of teenage Dr Jekyll and Mr Hyde. One minute Jo would be screaming abuse at her family, the next minute she'd be giggling on the phone with a girlfriend as if nothing had happened. Yet Jo knew her binges and tirades affected everyone in her family, "We don't get much food in the house 'cause I'd either not eat it or I'd just eat it all and then feel horrible and have a rage and they'd have to put up with me." Whenever there was food in the house, Michael and Julie would lie awake at night listening to Jo in the kitchen:

> She'd be cooking up a storm. And everything would go. All the food. She could go through a whole loaf of bread, a whole hot chicken, packets of biscuits, a whole box of cereal. By morning, everything would be gone. (Julie)

When Julie was cooking Jo would hover, desperately pestering Julie for something to eat as if she hadn't eaten for days. Julie knew the routine: the pestering was just the precursor to an uncontrollable binge. Once Julie's frustration got the better of her. She laughs when she thinks about it now but she was angry at the time. She whisked Jo's dinner away, walked down the hallway and flushed the food down the toilet, saying, "Let's just bypass the middle man, shall we?" In desperation, Michael and Julie started storing the food in their bedroom under lock and key.

Jo's self-destructive regime made concentrating hard and she struggled at school and through a succession of part-time jobs. Her existence revolved around food. The tension of living this way slowly built up. The next major crisis involved a cocktail of alcohol and over-the-counter drugs. Jo swallowed everything she could lay her hands on—painkillers, alcohol, and laxatives—and passed out on the beach. She was found by a local worker, who called an ambulance. The first Michael and Julie learned of the episode was when the police phoned from the hospital emergency room where Jo was having her stomach pumped. Jo was admitted to an eating disorders clinic but immediately ran away. At the time, Jo felt this move seemed like a powerful act of defiance but she didn't have any money and she was disorientated, frightened, and a long way from home. She ended up doubling back on her tracks until she was found by the clinic's security guards.

Jo's doctor and parents agreed that there was little point in trying to force Jo to stay at the clinic. The best option, they decided, was for Jo to go home but to see a psychiatrist regularly. Michael and Julie wasted no time in organizing a psychiatrist who was to be the first of so many psychiatrists, counselors, and therapists that Michael and Julie have lost count. Each time, Jo was difficult and uncooperative. She'd either throw a tantrum and storm out or sit in stony silence for an hour.

Within two years, Jo's body and social life were showing the strains of repeated abuse. She was too weak to play sport and dropped out of the surf club. Her knees were so sore from jogging and cycling that she struggled to walk. The ulceration and gastric bleeding from long-term laxative abuse gave her constant stomach pain, and the cuts she routinely inflicted on herself took longer and longer to heal as her system struggled with the effects of starvation. Jo tried to explain what was going on in her head when she was punishing and hurting herself:

> They can be little events that start and grow inside of you and build up until it just explodes. And it doesn't feel like me. It's not me doing it. It doesn't hurt when you're doing it. You just don't feel it, but when you wake up and you've got these cuts or burns on your arm they really do hurt. It's kind of like self-torture. You deserve it. You need this done to you—you've been bad. When I burned "fat" into my arm with matches, I think my parents had upset me and I didn't feel like I had lived up to what they wanted. I know that's stupid and I know it's not true but, at the time, it felt really, really awful—as if I hadn't turned out to what they had expected. It felt like I had gone down the wrong path and I'd destroyed the family. And that's when it happened.

Jo spent endless hours at night sitting on the computer scouring the internet for information about eating disorders and printing out screeds of pages. She trawled pro-ana websites and talked on chat lines with other people with eating disorders. She found lots of kindred spirits to confide in and to compare herself with. There were also plenty of allies from around the world who willingly shared their personal tips on how to lose weight and to purge.

Because she was awake all night on the internet, Jo spent most of her days sleeping. Jo invariably missed school, and when she did go she was either disruptive or worried that people were talking about her and left almost as soon as she'd arrived. Michael and Julie tried everything they could think of to change things. There were endless discussions, cajoling, negotiations, bribes, and even threats. They gave her sleeping pills to try and get her body clock back into sync but without success. They ferreted out people who had recovered from anorexia in the hope that one might connect with Jo and be able to help her. Nothing and no one seemed to be able to break through the barriers she had set up around herself.

---

## Box 6.2    Pro-ana Websites

Pro-ana (pro-anorexia) websites are internet sites set up and used by people with anorexia who do not want to recover. Pro-ana sites offer exercise and diet tips and online discussion forums where users can ask questions, share ideas, and meet other people who are pro-anorexia. Many pro-ana sites feature photos of emaciated women and celebrities. These photos are called "thinspiration" and can be edited to make the subject look even thinner.

Most sites agree that anorexia causes suffering and many also provide links to pro-recovery websites.[224] Nevertheless, pro-ana sites are intended for people who want to maintain and perfect their eating disorder. Consequently, many sites have a disclaimer denying all responsibility for the actions of users after they visit the sites. There has been extensive debate about whether pro-ana sites should be allowed to operate. Those wanting the sites banned have three main concerns:

- Vulnerable people will visit the sites and be exposed to information and attitudes that will trigger or worsen their eating disorders.
- Pro-ana sites foster undesirable competition and unhealthy weight-loss habits.
- The sites promote anorexia by portraying it as a valid lifestyle choice and even as a virtue akin to a religious quest.[225,226]

On the other side of the debate, users of the sites claim that they have the right to give and receive support from people like themselves.[227] They contend that the sites are pro-reality because they accept that some people do not recover from anorexia and provide a sympathetic, supportive community that is not available elsewhere.[224,228]

Even some non-users oppose banning pro-ana sites on the grounds that there is not yet enough research that the sites are harmful and that much of the pro-ana content is freely available on mainstream websites designed for "normal" dieters. They also argue that the popular media promotes thinness and weight obsession more powerfully than pro-ana sites. Banning pro-ana sites, they say, will only drive them underground and it is better to use the sites to understand their users.[224,229]

Pro-ana sites are widely accessed. Research suggests that around 40 percent of adolescents with eating disorders have visited a pro-ana site [230] but there has been limited investigation of the effects of such sites on users. In 2001, there were about 400 pro-ana sites but Yahoo! removed about 300 sites following pressure from eating disorder organizations and health providers.[231,232] Pro-ana users responded by starting a petition to allow pro-ana pages. By April 2005, the petition had more than 10,000 signatures.

Anti-anorexia activists have started using the same strategies as pro-ana sites to get their messages to individuals. One pro-recovery site disguises itself as a pro-ana site by using pictures of emaciated models in the hope of attracting people "who are looking for ways to stay in and suck their lives dry with this illness… I want to talk to people who go on the pro-ana sites…there's a desperate need for a reality check."[233]

After her third or fourth suicide attempt, Michael and Julie accepted that Jo was a danger to herself. On the advice of Jo's doctor, they agreed that she should be admitted to a hospital psychiatric ward overnight in the hope that this would scare her into reforming. Julie went with Jo to the hospital:

The doctor got the papers signed and spoke to the psychiatric unit to say this child would be coming over. The ambulance crew turned up and I went. I was terrified…the psychiatric unit is shocking. I was bloody terrified. I thought, "Oh my god." It was behind locked doors. I thought, "Hang on, what *are* we doing? Are we locking *us* in overnight or *her* overnight? Or are we just frightening her?" It was to give her a shock but at that point I wasn't quite aware of what was going on. I was dumbfounded… I'm trying to be all "Well, we're going to go here and they're going to reassess you and…" The ambulance crew has to sign you in and they can't leave until you have been looked after by the doctors at the psychiatric unit. And the doors lock. I think that frightened her for a moment. Just a moment. I was going berserk for a cigarette and I said to the person on the locked door, "I've got to have a cigarette." He said, "Just step outside for a minute." He let me out to have a cigarette and Jo went to go and he shut the door and said, "You sit down. You can't go." I thought she was going to explode but she didn't. She sat down quietly and I went back in with her. And the weirdest people would look at her. It was like fresh meat. I was terrified. I thought it was awful. I had said to her, "Jo, do you realize this is where we end up if you keep doing this?"… They left us there for about five or six hours…this is the sort of place that girls like her who keep committing—attempting suicide end up.

Throughout her trials, Jo leaned heavily on her younger brother, Sam. He was her source of strength, support, and comfort. Sam cuddled and consoled her when she was weeping with rage and pain and it was often Sam who found her when she'd collapsed from hunger or was drunk and delirious or had cut herself. Sam was also a stalwart for Julie and Michael. When Julie dissolved into tears at the strain and struggle of coping, it was Sam who reminded her that "Jo's ill. She can't help it." "He'd tap me on the shoulder and say, 'Don't forget, Mom, she is sick.' It would make you feel so good, and so sad at the same time." Jo knew her behavior was affecting Sam:

> My brother would get really upset 'cause he caught me vomiting or doing something, like taking laxatives. He couldn't have friends over because I'd either be having a fit or there wouldn't be food in the house to offer his friends or the house would be smashed up because I'd gone on a rage.

Inevitably, Jo's behavior seeped into Sam's view of the world. More often than they liked, Michael and Julie were summoned to meet with Sam's teachers because he'd breached some school rule. Concerned about his well-being, they suggested Sam see a therapist but he politely and firmly told them that he didn't need counseling—Jo was the one with the problems. Nevertheless, on his sixteenth birthday, Sam got drunk, smashed his car, and was arrested.

Jo felt responsible. She was convinced that Sam's accident was her fault because she'd failed to look after her brother. Distraught and upset, Jo "went absolutely crazy," smashing and throwing things in a destructive, uncontrolled release. She was so wild that Julie was frightened for her own safety and she locked herself in the bedroom and called the ambulance to take Jo to a secure hospital unit. Jo was released the next day and her doctors warned that further violence—including against herself—would mean being forcibly committed to a psychiatric unit for treatment. The caution fell on deaf ears. Soon after, Jo overdosed on antidepressants and over-the-counter painkillers:

> I was sick of everything. The malnutrition makes your head get pretty stuffed up and you don't think straight. I just got sick of everything. Everything seemed as though it was falling apart and nothing was working. At home was really crap. I was fighting with everyone and I had cut myself off from everyone and I just thought I don't need this. I can't

handle this. And I guess I was trying to take the easy way out. I thought if it happens then it happens. If I'm meant to die then I'm meant to die. If this works then it works.

This time Jo was admitted directly to a locked psychiatric ward. The admitting psychiatrist met with Jo, Julie, and Michael to work out a treatment plan. Jo was presented with two options. If she refused to enter into a program of medication and therapy, she'd stay in the psychiatric ward and be treated. If she agreed to treatment, Jo could be discharged and go home. Jo chose the latter option but it wasn't long before she started skipping sessions with her psychiatrist. In the end, he politely but firmly told her that he wouldn't waste appointments on someone who didn't turn up. Jo wasn't worried. At nearly 17 years of age, she figured that she was old enough to look after herself.

Michael and Julie eventually found another adolescent eating disorders clinic and Jo agreed to be admitted. They hoped this might be a fresh start but Jo announced that she had changed her mind as soon as they arrived at the clinic and wouldn't get out of the car. Short of physically dragging her kicking and screaming into the clinic, Michael and Julie felt incapable of doing anything and they turned around and went home. A few weeks later, Jo had a change of heart and asked her parents to take her to the clinic. From the beginning, however, Jo knew the clinic wasn't for her. Jo was thin but her weight had never dropped enough for her to be critically ill and she felt grossly overweight in a room full of girls who seemed thinner than herself. She became increasingly anxious and depressed and insisted on going home. Michael and Julie saw the clinic as their last hope but they knew Jo wouldn't cooperate if she didn't want to stay.

Even at the worst of times, the fun, affectionate daughter that Michael and Julie remember occasionally re-emerges. Jo chats to Julie about her friends, television shows, and life. She plays board games with Sam and cuddles and teases her father lovingly. But the last six years have been a torrid, emotional time. The strain has taken a toll on Julie's health. She survives by walking. The physical activity quells her angst:

> You cope but you're constantly anxious. I've developed irritable bowel syndrome. And there's that knotted feeling in your stomach. And you don't sleep. You're constantly worried about what she's doing. You're

always worried and you're constantly uptight and anxious. Always, always anxious.

Michael has found himself unexpectedly bursting into tears:

> I've never been a person who has been really emotional but I'd be driving on my own and I'd just start crying. There was nothing anyone could do for you and nothing anyone could do for her. Unless she wants to.

After years of living on a knife edge and much discussion with their counselor, Michael and Julie have decided to take a "tough love" approach to help Jo take responsibility for herself and to protect the well-being of everyone in their family. They've decided to stop giving in to intolerable behavior. No more driving for hours in the middle of the night to collect Jo when she is drunk. No more following her in the car and begging her to come home when she's run away. No more acquiescing during her destructive tantrums. No more "playing those sorts of games." The last time Jo went off her medication and refused counseling, they took the advice of Jo's eating disorders specialist and began the arduous legal process to put Jo under the control of a public guardian so that she could be treated against her wishes.

This move shocked Jo into taking her medication and seeing her doctor regularly. That was three months ago. Since then, Michael and Julie have seen positive changes although they're never exactly sure what triggers particular transformations. Nevertheless, Jo seems more conciliatory, responsible, and settled. Instead of venting her anger on her family, she's now lavishing love and attention on the new puppy she got for Christmas. Despite the disruption of the last few years, Jo graduated from high school and is now studying to be a nurse. She wants to help other people with eating disorders. She knows "you've got to help yourself before you can help other people" and this has motivated her to try and work towards recovery but she hasn't found it easy:

> Some days you think you're better. Then you have a couple of days when you seem to have stepped a million miles backward and are back to square one again. But I'm eating in front of people other than my family and my friends and my boyfriend. I don't have as many cuts all over me from hurting myself. It's been a long time since I've been admitted into hospital.

## Box 6.3   Compulsory Treatment

Compulsory treatment may be used when anorexia threatens a person's life or well-being. Compulsory treatment can mean forcibly confining a person to a treatment facility or imposing a particular type of treatment such as nasogastric feeding. Medico-legal, ethical, and psychological debates regarding the use of compulsory treatment for patients with anorexia are contentious and ongoing.[234-7] Most of the debate revolves around philosophical issues, the competence of people diagnosed with anorexia to refuse treatment, and the clinical implications of enforced treatment.

### Philosophical issues

In broad terms, two philosophical stances about medical care are relevant to the issue of compulsory treatment.[238] The "libertarian" stance views compulsory treatment as an infringement of a patient's rights and autonomy. It argues that individual free choice about treatment is a basic human right that should be protected even if that choice threatens an individual's well-being or survival or others do not agree with the choice. The "paternalistic" stance emphasizes a physician's "duty of care" to treat patients needing medical attention and holds that it is a moral and professional responsibility to provide treatment to those who are critically ill or near death, even if it is without the patient's consent. The relative emphasis on each philosophical stance in legislation, law, and professional practice varies between different states and countries.

### Competence

Competence is generally considered the capacity to give informed consent for treatment. The laws that allow young people to consent to treatment without their parents' or guardians' wishes vary by state and country but the provision for competence generally ranges from 12 to 18 years of age. Regardless of the legal constraints, establishing that someone with anorexia is competent and capable of making decisions about treatment is not straightforward. Some clinicians maintain that, by definition, being diagnosed with anorexia means that individuals are incompetent of making decisions about food and eating or judging the seriousness of their situation and the need to redress it.[234,239] In addition, physical starvation can cause irrationality, hostility, and delusions that diminish competence.[240] An alternative view is that it is discriminatory to assume that someone is incapable of making treatment decisions simply because they have anorexia. People diagnosed with anorexia may refuse treatment even when they understand their situation and are able to reason rationally.[239,241] On the other hand, people with anorexia may appear to have knowledge, understanding, and reasoning ability but other attitudes and values might mean they lack the competence to decide on treatment. For instance, patients may feel compelled by their anorexia to refuse treatment or they might see death or disability as less important than their anorexia and even as an accomplishment.[235]

### Clinical arguments

A central concern amongst clinicians is whether compulsory treatment is in the best interests of the person diagnosed with anorexia. The main arguments in favor of compulsory treatment are that there is no hard evidence that involuntary treatment is detrimental or leads to treatment rejection or worsening symptoms. Rather, compulsory treatment is viewed as evidence of the physician's devotion to the patient and is warranted when needed to save patients' lives or to protect their health, safety, and future physical development.[242]

Opponents of compulsory treatment argue that control and autonomy are central struggles for people diagnosed with anorexia and that these struggles will be compounded if health professionals take control by force.[240] They maintain that compulsory treatment is psychologically damaging, destroys trust, erodes the therapeutic relationship, and undermines the likelihood of further treatment being sought.[242,243] It produces resistance in patients and encourages them to battle against the professionals rather than cooperating with them to fight the anorexia. Given these conditions, opponents of compulsory treatment argue that any weight gained as a result of compulsory treatment is likely to be lost soon after discharge or will encourage bingeing or the use of undesirable methods of weight loss such as self-induced vomiting.[242]

Some patients have had very traumatic experiences with compulsory treatment and have described it in terms of imprisonment, punishment, and helplessness.[241] However, compulsory treatment is not a negative experience for everyone. Individuals who are struggling to be in control but feeling controlled by their anorexia can find that enforced treatment temporarily removes them from this dilemma.[82,130,240] Others report being grateful in hindsight that their treatment refusal was overridden or believing that enforced treatment was in their best interests.[241,244]

Compulsory treatment can be presented as a standard medical intervention when dangerous physical symptoms appear or as a penalty for non-compliance with other treatment programs and can be imposed with or without detailed and sensitive explanation, discussion, and counseling. These factors are likely to influence how an individual experiences and responds to compulsory treatment.[82]

Despite the traumas of the last six years, Michael and Julie remain loyal and committed to each other and to their children. They've drawn strength from a supportive network of friends, and seeing a counselor regularly has helped them to think through problems and learn not to blame themselves for what they can't control. They've survived by being able to laugh together, staying optimistic in the face of trauma, and knowing they can always count on each other. Despite everything they've been through, they still consider themselves fortunate:

> There are a few milestones in your lives. There's getting married, leaving the family in England, and coming out here. We really had no idea where we were going. We had to get a map to find out where this place was—so leaving home was a major time. Marriage, moving, and the birth of Jo and Sam are the key milestones by which I'd measure my life. They're the times that stand out. We used to sit down and say how lucky we were. I wouldn't say we've had a boring life but we've had a tranquil life compared to some of our friends dealing with separation, divorce, and so on. We still consider ourselves extremely, extremely lucky. Jo's a delight to be with at the moment. She really is. We don't have that aggressive nature anymore. She's fun to be with. (Michael)

# 7

# "Ahah, Anorexia Nervosa!"
## The Story of Antonia, Alice, Alan, and Aaron

Antonia has always been different from other children. She started school a year early and skipped a grade in elementary school. This year she got first place in five subjects and second in the other two. She's only 15 years old but she's already done her SAT tests. She scored in the 96th percentile and is waiting to hear if she's been awarded early admission to university. Her mother, Alice, is confident Antonia will be admitted. Antonia has always succeeded at anything she set out to do:

> We've yet to find out what she's not good at. She takes to languages. She speaks Italian like a native and she did that before she went to Italy [on a school exchange]. When she was four years old, she was taught by a former Olympian and he said she was good enough to go to the Olympics if she'd trained for swimming. With tennis, it was the same sort of thing. With dancing, she was winning awards but stopped when she was ten years old. (Alice)

Even though Antonia intends going to university—Alice says she'll do "a double or triple major in media and communications, film, and dance"—Antonia's plan is to become an actress. Her long ebony hair and heart-shaped face are captivatingly photogenic and she has the poise and confidence that an actress needs to hold an audience captive. Antonia's done debating and had a role in all theatrical productions at school. Alice is confident she'll get into acting school. But there's an age requirement for entry so Antonia will have to wait until she's 18 years old to do this.

Antonia and her mother, Alice, don't look alike but they *think* alike on most matters. Alice believes they have a telepathic connection. When Antonia was in Italy on a school exchange earlier in the year, Alice would sometimes get a strong sense that Antonia needed her:

She and I had a very strong psychic or a mental link. I would sometimes think, "I need to phone Antonia." I would stay up until it was one in the morning or three o'clock in the morning—whatever time it was when she would get home from school in Italy with the time difference—and I would phone and I'd say, "Okay, what's wrong?" And she'd say, "Nothing." I'd say, "Antonia, what's *wrong?*" And invariably something had happened. Not every time I phoned but they'd be little things. Just the sort of thing that she'd normally unload to me that obviously she's not going to unload to someone over there.

Antonia has two close friends at school but finds most of the other girls boring. Alice believes the other girls are intimidated by Antonia's intelligence:

She is younger than the kids in her year and so much smarter and she's had opportunities a lot of them hadn't had…a lot of the kids resent her because she got to go to Italy. Well, if their parents paid, they could go to Italy too… Antonia will use words that are perfectly normal for her but [the girls in her class say] "Could you say it in English?" And she thinks, "Well, I already downgraded it to your IQ level. I can't downgrade it any further. I don't know how." Because she's so much smarter, there's some resentment. They're put off by her. A little bit scared maybe. Even adults can find it difficult. Because she's so young, she's not supposed to have that knowledge and that ability. I think they find it a bit threatening or they see it as rude.

On the other hand, Antonia gets on well with adults. Alice describes her as a "favorite" with some of the teachers:

They love her. She's a teacher's delight so she is often in the staffrooms. If they've got morning tea or afternoon tea or they're having a lunch on, Antonia is always invited to have some and she'll stay and chat. Quite often she'll put food in the staffroom fridge and use their microwave and sometimes she'll stay there and eat.

Even as a baby, Antonia suffered from a sensitive digestive system and severe constipation. Alice fed her copious quantities of prune juice but the problem persisted even as Antonia got older and she found it particularly hard to digest carbohydrates like pasta, bread, and potatoes. Despite these problems, Antonia has a cosmopolitan palate. She hates junk food and prefers grilled rather than fried food, loves vegetables and fruit, and her favorite foods include exotic dishes like sushi, curries, octopus, and lobster. She has a weakness for calorie-loaded desserts like chocolate fudge, ice-cream, and lemon meringue pie. She'll even have the occasional glass of wine with her mother when they're at home.

Meals have always been casual and relaxed in their home. The family eats out regularly, and they rarely sit down to home-cooked meals together. Antonia and her younger brother, Aaron, are so busy with their different out-of-school activities that everyone comes and goes at different times. And they like different foods: Alan, Antonia's father, is a vegetarian; Alice will grab whatever's quick and easy to eat on the run; Aaron eats anything as long as it's smothered in ketchup; and Antonia is a self-confessed "grazer" who organizes her own meals.

Antonia's fifteenth birthday marked a turning point in her life. This was when she decided she was a "little bit overweight." She says her mother agreed but Alice doesn't remember this. Antonia didn't change her dinnertime routine but she did switch to eating only fruit and yoghurt during the day. Nevertheless, both mother and daughter agree that Antonia became more finicky when she got braces. She assiduously avoided eating anything that might get trapped in the wires—she hated it when this happened. When she progressed to a retainer, Antonia zealously followed the orthodontist's directive to steer clear of all and any sugar, even sweetened bread.

It was also when Antonia was 15 years old that Alice decided it was time to tell her that she had been sexually abused when she was 2 years old. The two boys involved were only 10 and 12 years old at the time and details of the incident are vague. Alice and Alan had been warned that Antonia might have repressed memories of the incident that could resurface as she got older. Alice had also started to notice that Antonia would sometimes get agitated when someone stood too close to her:

> We were told that she could remember when she got her period or her first sexual contact or at puberty. You know, like at any point…so given that she was going to Italy and there were these signs, I felt that she had to be told because I wasn't going to be there and I certainly didn't want to be telling her over the phone.

Alice wanted her daughter to have a chance to come to terms with this murky part of her past before she went away from her family. Although

Alice fretted and worried, Antonia was unperturbed by the news—the incident was too vague and distant.

---

### Box 7.1    Facts and Fictions of Sexual Abuse

The narratives of some women suggest that childhood sexual abuse played a part in the development of their eating disorder.[51] It is estimated that around 30 percent of people with eating disorders have experienced childhood sexual abuse. While the majority of people with eating disorders have not experienced childhood sexual abuse, this rate is towards the higher end of estimates for the general population, which range from 17 to 33 percent.[245-7] The rate of reported childhood sexual abuse amongst people with eating disorders is similar to that amongst people with other psychiatric disorders, such as depression. This pattern suggests that childhood sexual abuse may be a risk factor for psychiatric problems generally rather than eating disorders specifically.[248]

While most studies have looked at the rates of childhood sexual abuse amongst mixed groups of people with eating disorders, only four studies to date have compared the frequency of childhood sexual abuse amongst women with anorexia and "healthy" women. Of these, only one study found childhood sexual abuse to be more common in women with anorexia. This study was based in the UK and compared 40 women with anorexia and 40 "healthy" women.[249] Studies from Sweden and Japan, involving respectively 37 and 73 women with anorexia and larger control groups of women without anorexia, found no significant differences in childhood sexual abuse between women with anorexia and those without.[250,251] In a Canadian study involving 28 women with anorexia, childhood sexual abuse was not significantly more common amongst women with anorexia than amongst a healthy comparison group of 24 women without anorexia but childhood sexual abuse was more common amongst the 12 women with the binge-purge subtype of anorexia.[252] With some exceptions,[250] studies that have compared the rates of childhood sexual abuse amongst people with different symptom patterns have found that reports of childhood sexual abuse amongst people who binge and purge are more frequent than amongst those with restricting anorexia.[245,248,253]

The impact of sexual abuse on victims is complex and likely to be affected by many factors including interpersonal skills, family relationships, and the reactions of others to the abuse.[248,249] Research is needed on how childhood sexual abuse interacts with other factors and plays a role in the development and maintenance of anorexia for some people.

---

It was also when she was 15 years old that Antonia went on her four-month sojourn in Italy. The time unlocked new freedoms. She relished the culture and traveled with her host family to Spain as well as around Italy. She also had her first holiday romance. Alice chuckles as she remembers:

> She phoned me the next morning and she told me she had had her first French kiss, from a French boy. And I said, "Did he try anything else?" And she said, "Well, he tried to put his hand under my top, but there was no way!" I said, "And what did you think of the French kiss?" She said, "It was absolutely gross, all that saliva, yuck!"

### Box 7.2    Anorexia in Cultural and Ethnic Groups

Until recently, anorexia was thought to be an illness that was limited to Caucasian women in affluent western countries and it was assumed that other cultural groups were immune from anorexia. Research now suggests that anorexia and other eating disorders exist in many non-western countries and in most ethnic minorities in western countries.[21,75,254]

The conventional explanation for the existence of eating disorders in non-western countries is increased exposure to western ideals of thinness, especially as a result of global media.[255] However, researchers have suggested that other factors might contribute, such as modernization, urbanization, increased affluence and consumerism, erosion of traditional values, and greater opportunities for women's education, autonomy, and workplace involvement.[256-8] Local cultural values and practices can also promote eating disorders. Traditionally, for example, slenderness is highly valued amongst Japanese women. In China, food is used as a form of communication, reward, punishment, and to influence others' behavior.[259] Some studies have found that women living in non-western countries like Iran and Taiwan had higher levels of body dissatisfaction and eating disturbances than their countrywomen living in western countries, suggesting that exposure to western culture may not be a key factor.[260] The influence of western thin ideals will also depend on their adoption and interpretation by particular individuals and communities. For example, in Belize a high value is placed on looking after oneself and one's bodily needs so the idea of restricting food to be thin is generally not seen as sensible.[261]

Studies that have investigated eating disorders and disturbances amongst cultural minorities in western countries report mixed findings. Some have found that particular ethnic minorities are at lower risk of eating pathology than the cultural majority and suggest that this is due to lower levels of acculturation or adherence to mainstream values, attitudes, and identities. However, other studies have found that migrants from non-western backgrounds actually had more eating pathology than Caucasian controls.[260] Feminist scholars propose that eating disorders are more common when women have no clear sense of identity, for example, as they try to negotiate differences between cultures and values or to fit in with a new society.[258]

Much of our knowledge and beliefs about anorexia are based on research and clinical work with Caucasian women in developed, western countries. Researchers have questioned its relevance for other cultural groups.[262] For example, fear of fat is a diagnostic criterion for anorexia but research in some Asian and African populations has found that anorexia frequently exists without fear of fat.[16,263] In Ghana, for example, where there is little pressure to be thin, self-starvation still occurs but has religious meanings related to self-control and denial of hunger.[264] In Belize, the desire to be thin is rare and not related to beauty ideals but to a perception that it is necessary for upward social mobility or job success, especially in the tourism industry.[261] Likewise, the reasons that immigrants and non-white people in countries like the US are vulnerable to eating disorders are thought to be different from the reasons for eating disorders in the dominant culture. For example, African-American and Hispanic American women have described their eating problems as ways of coping with stressful social conditions like poverty, class, and racism.[75,265]

The rate of anorexia and other eating disorders amongst different cultural groups is difficult to pinpoint because most studies use instruments developed for western populations and these may be culturally inappropriate.[21,262,266] It is clear, however, that anorexia has an almost global presence though its meanings and manifestations may vary between ethnic and cultural groups.

Antonia's stay in Italy was also a time of new constraints. For the first time, Antonia became conscious of her body. In her social circle in Italy, weight and appearance seemed to be a critical concern. Antonia had always been relaxed about her weight and figured that about 45 kilos was an ideal weight given that she was 150 centimeters tall. However, the young teenager was very upset when she overheard her host mother critically commenting to others about the amount of weight Antonia had put on since she'd arrived.

At home, Antonia always ate what she wanted when she wanted. In Italy, meals were at designated times and were long, lavish occasions, bursting with pasta and bread. For the first time Antonia found she "had very little control over what I was eating and I'd come from a family where I'd always had control." Antonia's Italian couldn't keep up with the fast flow of the mealtime conversations and she ate to occupy herself during the prolonged meals. As her language skills improved, she talked more and ate less. Eventually, Antonia's host mother was so worried about the rapidity of Antonia's weight loss that she started weighing Antonia's breakfast cereal and sitting beside her in the mornings until she ate every scrap.

Despite these efforts, Antonia was so thin by the time she arrived home that Alice walked past her three times at the airport before recognizing her. Despite Antonia's weight loss, both mother and daughter insist that Antonia was not *thinking* or *behaving* like an "anorexic" at the time. This change happened during their family holiday in the weeks that followed. Although Antonia had never fussed about food or exercise, she decided she wanted to keep off the weight she'd lost in Italy. Now she began skipping meals and started working out in the hotel gym to offset the calories she knew she'd consume at the next meal. Her initial idea wasn't to lose weight, "I just didn't want to gain it." However, the increased control over *what* she ate slid imperceptibly into controlling how *much* she ate. In Antonia's words, "It just snowballed into this obsessive desire."

By the time the holiday was over, Antonia weighed only 35 kilos. When the family doctor diagnosed anorexia Antonia was shocked: "You never think you're going to become anorexic." The pronouncement suddenly prodded her into admitting that her thinking about food had become a "skewed pattern." Antonia dates her decision to "fight her anorexia" from that moment.

Alice took Antonia to see a specialist in adolescent eating disorders. Because Antonia's body mass index was only 15.3, the specialist wanted to admit her to hospital immediately. Alice resisted. She thought it would be psychologically and emotionally damaging for Antonia to be admitted straightaway. Besides, Antonia had to complete exams at school. The specialist acquiesced and agreed to monitor Antonia's weight for a few weeks. Antonia stopped doing any exercise, attended her weekly check-ups at the hospital, and she and her mother joined a support group for parents and people with anorexia. Alice felt this was worthwhile:

> It was good for both of us. One of the things is that it's really nice when you find out you're not the only one. In the support group alone, you know, they're recovering or have recovered for several years. So you find that you're not the only one and there is life after it. And I think that's really important. And you can express whatever you want to express—not just assuming that what you're being told is right or that what you're thinking is right.

Antonia also followed the diet recommended by the dietician but it wasn't always easy. At times, the carbohydrate-rich menu seemed to trigger bloating, stomach cramps, and constipation. Antonia and Alice feel that the fact that they've persisted with the diet is testimony to Antonia's determination to get better:

> She'll lie down on my bed and she'll say, "Will you rub my stomach?" She'll lie on my bed and the tears are rolling down her cheeks…not every morning but five out of seven mornings. And she will often get me to take her for a drive for an hour because she just finds it easier to cope with the car moving because of feeling so bloated. She will draw her legs up and sometimes she's just sobbing in agony, crying. (Alice)

Things haven't been easy at home either. Life is organized around Antonia. Her parents are so concerned for her well-being that they find it impossible to refuse her anything. It doesn't matter what: a late night drive to soothe her stomach, an unplanned dash to buy an out-of-season mango, or a jar of her favorite jam. Antonia's behavior towards Aaron has also changed. She yells at him without apparent cause, reducing Aaron to sobs and requiring Alice to step in to stop a full-scale meltdown. Antonia has also become strangely intolerant of noise. Even the sound of the television, barely audible behind closed doors at the other end of the house, causes her intense pain. More than once Alice and Alan have had to deploy elaborate ruses to get Aaron to abandon his favorite television show and out of the house so Antonia can have peace and quiet. The fact that Antonia can eat whatever and whenever she wants has made it very difficult to instill the idea of a balanced diet in Aaron. The strain has been reflected in Alice's relationship with Aaron and she confesses to yelling at him for silly, unwarranted reasons.

To help Alice, Alan has taken up most of the domestic work. He ferries Aaron to and from school and sports practice and takes him bike riding so that Antonia and Alice can have "quality" time together. Alan "is not a person who really expresses emotions" but the stress has affected his health and manifested itself in chronic sinusitis and headaches. For Alan, the primary challenge has been to find the right balance in dealing with his daughter and her illness. Alice doesn't feel he always manages to get it right, but admits that it isn't always easy:

> At times he's been very obtuse—for want of a better description—or thoughtless. He can be *so* understanding and *so* considerate and *so* good about lots of things. And then, every now and again, at the worst possible moment, he will say something inappropriate or thoughtless. Like, Antonia and I will have been out and had afternoon tea so Antonia doesn't want to eat [dinner] at six o'clock. Well, he says, "Oh, you've got to eat! You're anorexic. You've got to eat!" Antonia gets upset because he's being inconsiderate—which he is—but it's also because there's this huge emphasis on food and partly [sigh] because you don't know what to say. Nothing's right, you know?

As for Alice, she's sick of having life constantly revolve around food. She's so busy and exhausted looking after Antonia that her own health care has suffered. She knows she needs to watch her diet and lose weight but she's too exhausted to think about this. Too often, she settles for corn chips and dip for dinner—at least it's easy. Alice loves her children but she never wanted to be a stay-at-home mother and has always worked. She's bitter about being made to feel guilty by people who try to find the root of Antonia's anorexia in the way Alice has raised her: the fact that she didn't breastfeed and returned to work after Antonia was born, or that she encouraged Antonia to start school early and skip a grade, or allowed her to go to Italy by herself when she was so young. Alice tries to be philosophical:

> I don't think it really matters what decisions you make, people manage to say, if you hadn't done this or if you'd done that, then maybe things would be better.

Despite Antonia's resolve to recover and her efforts to stick to her new diet, within a few weeks of the first visit to the specialist Antonia's weight had dropped to 32 kilos and she'd stopped menstruating. At her specialist's insistence, Antonia has been admitted to hospital, placed on a rigid diet of supported meals, and is being artificially fed through a nasogastric tube.

Although Antonia has acquiesced, she's angry. She feels cheated because she did everything the doctor and dietician told her to do, including eating the carbohydrate-heavy diet "at the expense" of her preferred foods. Yet, for some inexplicable reason, she's failed to put on weight. Antonia is also upset by being put on artificial feeding. She didn't expect this and doesn't like it. It makes her feel sick, bloated, and too full to eat the hospital meals or have room for the food she wants, like chocolate milkshakes from the cafeteria.

Antonia believed she had anorexia when she was first diagnosed. Now she's not so sure. She's spent time searching the internet and wonders if she has some other illness because she doesn't have classically "anorexic" symptoms. She's distressed by her emaciation: "I don't look at myself and see myself as fat. I look at myself and think—you know those pictures you see of people who have been in war, you know those concentration camps. That's what I see." Alice agrees: "She looks at herself and she cries." Antonia contrasts herself with the girls with anorexia in the hospital ward and has decided she thinks and behaves differently. She's tried to put on weight and can't, but they're just interested in losing more weight. She loves food but these girls do everything they can to avoid eating. At mealtimes they just "stare at their food as if it's going to jump up off the plate and attack them."

However, Antonia can't convince the staff that she's different. She knows the other girls breach the rules by bingeing, vomiting, and throwing away food and she resents being tarred with the same brush. She's being honest and doing all the right things and feels the staff should trust her. Surely if the staff believed her they would give her more freedom and treat her differently?

> They look at you, the nurses and staff, as if they're trying to figure out when you're lying—which I'm not—but you still get those looks, it makes you feel like less than a human being. Like you don't deserve to be trusted.

What galls Antonia most is the sense that she's being treated as an anorexia stereotype rather than as an individual. She's tried to convince her doctors that she has always been blighted by poor circulation and constipation but feels her explanations are ignored. It's the same story in her dealings with other health professionals:

> I did see a psychologist and I don't plan on seeing him again. He reads things into the fact that everyone in my family has a name that starts with A: Alice, Aaron, Antonia, and Alan. With me it was a fluke. I would have been Helen if my father hadn't objected because he had a cousin he didn't like with that name. So I was called Antonia. It just happened to be a name that started with an A. And then my brother came along. We had three As so we weren't going to name him Stephen or John and have him be the odd one out. So yes, it was intentional to give my brother a name starting with A. But this psychologist reads all sorts of things into that about co-dependency issues and so on…it just frustrates me trying to convince someone who will, in the end, remain unconvinced that there's no deep meaning behind the fact that our names all begin with A.

At first Alice also accepted the diagnosis of anorexia. Now she's skeptical. She can't understand how Antonia can have anorexia given the amount she eats:

> Last Friday night, she and Alan went to the Indian restaurant and Alan said when he got home, "I still feel nauseous from the amount of food your daughter put away. She ate more than me." Saturday night—yet again—we went out and she had salad and she had a lot of seafood and she went back for her second plate of dessert. Alan and I just looked at each other and Alan said, "She has eaten more than I have. In fact, I think she's eaten more than you and I combined." We were feeling ill at the quantity. She had seafood, she had about a quarter of my chicken. She had fruit. She had some pasta. She had two desserts. She had potato—she did have some potato. I mean, she just keeps going back for more… I cannot watch her eat this, I just literally cannot see this. It's too much food for me, you know. And this is several times a week that we have these big meals.

Alice also knows that Antonia doesn't purge or exercise. She's spent a lot of time with Antonia at restaurants and they have visited the ladies' washroom together, and she's stayed up at night and listened at the bathroom and bedroom doorways to make sure. Alice is confident she'd know if Antonia was doing anything she shouldn't and she doesn't like constantly checking on her daughter:

> I feel guilty about her being watched all the time and guilty that I'm part of that. I know that she's an honest kid because she's so upfront with me, and it doesn't come naturally to me to be watching her and being mistrustful of her.

---

## Box 7.3   The Experience of Hospitalization

Hospitalization can be a difficult experience. The following issues have been identified as especially significant for people hospitalized for anorexia.

### Choice and autonomy

People with anorexia value control but hospitalization takes away control.[137] The decision for hospitalization is usually made by doctors and parents and this may be made against the wishes of the person diagnosed with anorexia. Individuals may find that they have limited autonomy in hospital. They are expected to follow hospital routines and meal plans and to put on weight in order to be discharged or to access hospital privileges. Some people resist the loss of control by disputing their diagnosis, questioning clinicians' competence, refusing to comply with treatment, or secretly undermining treatment by hiding food or artificially inflating their weight. Others use strategies like crying, flirting, and complaining to try to influence doctors' treatment decisions.

### Labeling and monitoring

In hospital, individuals are closely monitored to ensure that they comply with their treatment and meal program. This regime can make people feel mistrusted and typecast. However, when people diagnosed with anorexia are treated as individuals, hospitalization can be a positive experience and staff are appreciated.[85]

### The stigma of psychiatry

Being hospitalized for a psychiatric condition can be a traumatizing experience. Family and friends can react negatively to the stigma of mental illness and people treated in general psychiatric wards may be fearful of patients with other psychiatric conditions.[85]

---

## Isolation

Hospital can be a lonely experience. Children and adolescents being treated for anorexia often find it especially difficult to be separated from their parents and families, particularly if the staff are unfamiliar or if there is no one in their ward of a similar age or with the same diagnosis.

## The emphasis on food

In hospital, food is a medical intervention. A primary purpose of hospitalization is weight gain and hospital routines are structured around refeeding. Consequently, some people diagnosed with anorexia complain that the organization of meals, the unappetizing nature of hospital food, and the quantities they have to eat further reduce the appeal of food. They also struggle with the dissonance between a hospital regime of eating large portions of full fat foods and social messages about health, beauty, and the desirability of being thin outside hospital.

## The emphasis on weight

Weight gain is a primary goal of hospitalization and a measure of treatment success[87] but patients report that their anorexic thoughts and feelings, such as depression and body hatred, remain unchanged or are worsened if there is a lack of attention to emotional and psychological issues in hospital.[137]

## An anorexic identity

Because of the emphasis on food and weight and the lack of other diversions, people with anorexia report that their thoughts in hospital can be consumed by their anorexia. The company of other people with anorexia can encourage anorexia as a topic of thought and conversation, provide a source of new information about anorexic strategies, and foster competition to see who is the "best" anorexic.[85] However, some patients have reported that hospitalization has moved them to recovery by jolting them into an awareness of the seriousness of their condition and its impact on their lives.[137]

Alice has also scoured the internet for information on anorexia and for different diseases involving extreme weight loss. She's found a string of them:

Addison's disease, Crohn's disease, upper something arterial disease, cancer, poisoning, parasites, worms, gall bladder disease, various things that I can't even begin to pronounce can cause anorexia…as well as celiac disease, carbohydrate intolerance, parasites.

Like Antonia, Alice has come to believe that her daughter's anorexia is atypical and may mask some mysterious, unidentified illness. In her view, Antonia's "anorexia" and "nervosa" are two distinctly different problems and they need to be addressed separately. On the one hand, Alice sees anorexia as "purely weight loss" and insists that the standard diagnostic criteria for anorexia can't apply to Antonia because she doesn't starve or purge or have a distorted body image or a fear of fat. On the other hand, Alice sees the tears and emotional outbursts that have accompanied Antonia's weight loss as symptomatic of "nervosa" but figures this behavior is easily explained by recent events in Antonia's life: her desire to do well in her exams, to get early admission to university, and by the news that she was sexually abused as a child.

Alice has voiced her views to Antonia's clinicians and is exasperated by their skepticism and apparent disinterest in searching for alternative explanations for Antonia's condition. Alice feels she's been categorized as a "difficult mother" and that her family has been pigeon-holed as a stereotypical "anorexic" family.

> It's just infuriating and frustrating. You just want to get their heads and strangle them! There's a really big part of both Antonia and I that desperately want her to have something else wrong with her… Just to be able to shove it down their throats and say, "See? We told you. We told you from the word go that there was something else going on. You should have listened in the first place instead of just saying, 'Oh, you're a parent and you don't know. You don't understand. We deal with this all the time. We know better than you.' If you had listened to us in the first place, then this would've been fixed sooner."
>
> Her father and I are not complete idiots. On the one hand, you have people saying, "We're the specialists," "We're the physicians." On the other hand, you know your child and you're the one with them all the time. Just because she's a teenage girl and lost weight they say, "Ahah, anorexia nervosa!" One plus one equals 41. If a girl is in any way different or she's got any stresses on her, like if she's doing more subjects at school or applying to university, there's just this automatic assumption that the pressure has caused anorexia.

## Box 7.4 Challenges of Diagnosing Anorexia

Diagnosing anorexia is not always straightforward and the difficulties increase when individuals do not acknowledge their eating problems, hide their weight loss, or maintain that they have particular reasons for not eating such as stomach pain, nausea, food intolerances, or lack of appetite. When a medical explanation is sought, these behaviors can cause the anorexia to be misdiagnosed as symptomatic of another illness. Conversely, an illness that causes weight loss can be mistaken for anorexia, particularly if someone's characteristics, history, or environment appear stereotypically "anorexic."[267,268]

However, when weight loss is the result of a physical illness, the individual does not usually exhibit the psychological features of anorexia such as excessive concern with body weight or shape and the desire to lose more weight.[7,269] Some medical problems, however, can cause behaviors that mimic anorexia such as willful food avoidance, vomiting, excessive exercise, and increased irritability.[270,271]

The medical literature and personal accounts document a variety of medical illnesses that have been mistaken for anorexia including: gastrointestinal disorders such as celiac disease, inflammatory bowel disease, gall bladder disease and Crohn's disease; endocrine disorders like hyperthyroidism and Addison's disease; central nervous system disorders such as brain or spinal tumors; cancer; infections like AIDS and Lyme disease; and parasites like tapeworm.[267,271-4]

People who have been misdiagnosed lament that non-standard tests like stool tests, ultrasounds, x-rays, or intestinal tract tests were not performed earlier.[275] On the other hand, some people with anorexia have reported being tested for or diagnosed with a wide variety of medical problems before an accurate diagnosis was received. Consequently, it has been argued that extensive testing can delay intervention and reinforce denial by people diagnosed with anorexia or their families.[276]

Treatment for other problems can have a negative impact on someone with anorexia. For example, a diagnosis of food allergy can provide a rationale for further food restriction,[269] while attempts to treat problems associated with anorexia with medical interventions fail to address the underlying eating problem. The absence of a speedy diagnosis can mean the anorexia is more severe or chronic by the time an appropriate intervention is accessed.

Alice also objects that the hospital imposes the same rules on everyone. Before Antonia was admitted to hospital, Alice spent a lot of time describing to her the minutiae of hospitalization, the sort of medication she would encounter, the tests and procedures that would be performed. Nevertheless, Alice resents that Antonia's admission seemed so speedy and perfunctory. She thinks it's important for families to have more time—"a week or so"—to come to terms with the idea of hospitalization so girls have the time to be spoiled, to do last minute shopping and "a chance to cry to Mom."

> So she can have time to think: What books do I want to take? What CDs? To put things around the hospital bed and think of hospitalization in a more positive way. To give us time to come to terms with it.

Alice also objects to the expectations placed upon Antonia on the ward. Like the other patients, Antonia is expected to attend the hospital school. Alice believes an exception should be made for Antonia because she's already done her SATs and is on the verge of being accepted for university. Alice's angry that the hospital seems insistent on "treating Antonia like a child just because she has anorexia."

At this point, it's not clear how Antonia and Alice's story will end. Antonia is still losing weight and both she and her mother remain convinced that there's a more sinister physical problem at play. At least at the moment, the family is at a crossroad and the future is uncertain. Alice is weighing up the possibilities of moving Antonia to another hospital if her current doctors refuse to "keep an open mind" about the nature of Antonia's illness and how she should be treated on the ward.

# 8

# "It Can Happen to the Nicest Families"
## The Story of Ruth, Beth, David, and Callum

Ruth is a cheerful, lively little girl with flashing eyes and a wide, captivating grin. She's got a cheeky sense of humor and can always make her family laugh with her funny impersonations of her school teachers. Until she was ten years old, Ruth had little interest in sport or exercise. She was a real "lounge lizard" who loved eating and lazing in front of the television. All this changed when she began dance classes. Ruth looked around the class and all she could see were "skinny" girls. Although Ruth was slim and petite, she felt fat and self-conscious, particularly in the body-hugging leotard the dance class had to wear. Ruth ached to look just like all the other girls and, in an effort to recast her figure, she embarked on a fitness campaign. She began by cutting out junk food, chocolates, and the desserts that she'd always loved, and by doing a bit more exercise—nothing significant, just practicing her dance routines and riding her bike.

There were other changes when the family moved from the middle of a bustling suburb to a large, new house set on five acres just outside of town. Ruth and her younger brother, Callum, would spend hours riding their bikes, combing the property in search of treasure and hunting imaginary monsters in the nearby forest. Ruth loved the unfettered freedom of being outdoors and she became addicted to the exhilaration of running through the dark forest and open meadows where only the trees and birds were witnesses to her presence.

Ruth pursued her fitness campaign and quickly lost her puppy fat. Her parents, Beth and David, were proud of her determination to get fit and healthy and saw this as a positive lifestyle move, and Ruth reveled in the flurry of compliments from family and friends. Even though other people thought she looked "just right," Ruth didn't feel as if she could relax. The idea of easing up and possibly losing her new, slender shape was intolerable. She didn't make a conscious decision to restrict her eating further or intensify her exercise routine. The shift crept up so gradually that no one realized.

---

### Box 8.1    Healthism

In western societies, a thin body is equated with being fit and healthy and it is considered an individual's responsibility to be healthy and, therefore, thin. This phenomenon is called "healthism."[163] Healthism messages are evident in medical literature, in the media (e.g. the "obesity epidemic"), in schools (e.g. the health curriculum), and in advertising. Healthism messages are used to promote and justify powerful industries that market weight-loss programs, diet books, slimming drugs, and even cosmetic surgery.[277]

As a result of the alignment of health and thinness, being thin has come to be viewed as a morally responsible lifestyle choice.[183,277] In movies and on television, women who achieve success, love, and happiness are invariably thin and the diet and exercise industries promote thinness as a ticket to self-esteem and well-being.[278,279] Consequently, thinness has come to be viewed as a desirable moral attribute and essential for a happy and successful life.

Healthism presents the causal link between thinness and health as an indisputable fact and studies that link obesity to ill health and death are well publicized.[280] Yet other research suggests that people who are overweight are not necessarily at increased risk for illness and death and that even obese people can be healthy if they are fit and active.[281,282]

A correlation between illness and high body weight does not necessarily mean that illness is caused by weight rather than other factors such as genetics, sedentary lifestyles, weight cycling ("yo-yo dieting"), and health-care discrimination.[283,284] Moreover, the benefits of weight loss have been contested. There is considerable evidence that deliberate weight loss is rarely maintained in the long term and that dieting, especially chronic dieting, can have negative psychological effects.[208,285] Some studies have suggested that weight loss can actually increase the risk of mortality.[286,287] The view that good health can be achieved through good nutrition and physical exercise rather than by dieting or being a particular weight is rarely heard in the current "war against fat."[124,125] Yet, because healthism messages equate health with body weight, they can encourage the use of unhealthy weight-loss strategies, such as crash diets, smoking, and drugs.[288,289]

In cultures where thinness is equated with beauty and fat is equated with ugliness, healthism messages are rarely questioned because it is taken for granted that attractiveness and health are linked.[124,290] While the promotion of thinness as beautiful is criticized as contributing to anorexia, the promotion of thinness as healthy can be an equally powerful but negative force because it is sanctioned by medicine and has moral overtones. Many girls with anorexia have described their eating problems as beginning with a determination to get healthy or said that being thin made them feel virtuous rather than greedy and lazy.[163] Many people with anorexia worry that if they start to eat normally they will get fat and healthism messages emphasize that being overweight is something to be feared. An alternative is to view a healthy lifestyle as important regardless of weight and to avoid judging people's health based on their appearance.

Throughout the cold winter months, Beth and David had only seen Ruth warmly rugged in layers of clothes. Their illusions were shattered when summer arrived and the family went on holidays to the beach. Beth first realized the extent of Ruth's weight loss when they went shopping for Ruth's new swimsuit. When she saw Ruth's emaciated body for the first time in the change room, Beth was so horrified that she felt physically ill.

Living together in the close confines of their small holiday apartment revealed another disturbing pattern. Beth and David discovered that Ruth's desire to get fit had transformed into an all-consuming compulsion to exercise. Ruth would eat a scant breakfast and then refuse to leave the apartment until she'd done 45 minutes of exercise. She'd insist on going for a run after lunch and dinner would always be followed by more exercise routines, dancing, or running.

As a medical doctor, David blames himself for not noticing earlier. He felt his training and experience should have alerted him to the signs. He tried cajoling, bribing, and chastising but nothing seemed to make a difference. Trying to pressure Ruth to eat more or exercise less just provoked battles and screaming tantrums that left everyone in the family feeling exhausted and upset. For David, coming face to face with anorexia was personally and professionally confronting. It challenged his identity as a doctor and made him question his parenting skills. He bemoaned the absence of a section on "the anorexic child" in the "parenting manual":

> It's been a bit strange because there's the doctor *me* and the father *me*. It's one thing being a father and having a child [who is] potentially lethally ill and being able to do very little to intervene short of coming down heavy on her. So from a father's point of view, it's very frustrating. But it's probably more frustrating being a doctor because to her I'm not a doctor. It's hard to actually be a doctor and a father at the same time—to see what she needs to be able to do but then to see that she can't do it because her perception of what's going on is different from mine. That's very frustrating. You can see this person becoming more emaciated, tired, lethargic, her personality changing. And you can't do something to change it. It's hard as a parent and as a doctor. What sort of role do I play? Can I mix the two? Should I just be a father? Certainly couldn't just be a doctor. But it's hard to divorce the two. That was my dilemma.

As soon as they returned from holidays, David took Ruth to see a pediatrician specializing in eating disorders. Ruth's weight had dropped to 32 kilos, she was clinically depressed, her ankles were purple and swollen from all the exercise, and cardiac failure looked imminent. A few days after her eleventh birthday, Ruth was admitted to hospital where she was sedated, put on bed rest, and fed through a nasogastric tube.

Ruth only has negative memories of this time. There were two other girls with anorexia in the ward and the trio gravitated together but Ruth found herself isolated and alone when her compatriots left. The other children in the ward didn't understand anorexia and made it clear that they thought Ruth's compulsion to avoid food and eating was "weird." Ruth's loneliness was amplified by the hospital's policy of restricted parental visits and her inability to build a positive rapport with many of the clinical staff. Ruth had starved herself and over-exercised but she'd never vomited or used laxatives. Yet she felt the staff assumed that everyone with anorexia behaved in the same way and so she felt pressured to fit into their notion of anorexia. She came to the conclusion that the staff weren't interested in the girls as individuals and therefore they didn't *really* care about their well-being. Ruth concluded that the nurses were "really mean," the doctor "wasn't good...he didn't really solve any problems," and the psychologists "just didn't like us so they didn't really follow through."

Beth also struggled to come to terms with the hospital's policy of restricted visits and the rigid regime that both patients and parents had to follow. Beth's only desire was to be with Ruth—to reassure and comfort her and to make sure she was all right. While Beth was struggling to come to terms with Ruth's diagnosis and hospitalization, she felt blamed for her daughter's condition:

> We were treated like we'd been bad parents. The nursing staff in particular had no empathy for either us or Ruth. There were a couple of nice ones but on the whole they were extremely cold. They seemed to have no understanding of what it was like to put your 11-year-old daughter in hospital and then be given restricted visiting. They couldn't stand in my shoes for just a minute. It was so regimented. When it's mealtime [they said], "You can go home now." When we wanted to have a little bit of privacy and I pulled the curtains around her cubicle to give her a cuddle, the nurse came in and ripped them back and said, "You're not allowed to do this." They felt that we had to be watched at all times. It made me angry.

As for David, he found it increasingly difficult to be "just a parent" when he was dealing with other doctors. He was used to being respected for his medical expertise, speaking his mind, and being heard. The hospital's philosophy was that parents and clinical staff should work together as a team but Beth and David felt pressured to "blandly and blindly" support the clinicians' decisions even if they disagreed.

It was six weeks before the hospital agreed that Ruth was sufficiently physically stable to be discharged. As far as Beth and David were concerned, the post-discharge follow-up from the hospital was "just a bit of a check-up and on your way." Unsure of how to deal with a daughter who was physically out of danger but still wrestling with anorexic thoughts and desires, Beth and David felt as if they were left floundering. The months that followed were a blur of frustration as they hunted for people who might be able to help Ruth. They tried different counselors and dieticians but none seemed to know anything about anorexia or how it should be handled. The search for a psychiatrist or psychologist was just as futile. Their approaches ranged from "How's she going? Good. Okay" to weeks of chatting amiably with Ruth about nothing of consequence in the hope that she'd eventually open up and reveal *why* she had anorexia. None of these paths struck Beth and David as either productive or helpful.

## Box 8.2   Challenges in Treating Anorexia

Clinicians involved in treating an adolescent with anorexia may include doctors, nurses, dieticians, psychologists, social workers, counselors, occupational therapists, and physiotherapists. Which clinicians are involved in any case of anorexia will depend on the needs of the individual at the time, the treatment setting, and the availability and affordability of clinical expertise.

### Challenges in working with people with anorexia

People with anorexia are often described as uncooperative and difficult to treat because they do not acknowledge their diagnosis or the need for treatment and they sabotage or drop out of treatment.[291,292] Clinicians can experience failure, frustration, stress, helplessness, and exhaustion when individuals are openly or covertly resistant and clinicians can sometimes feel that they are forcing treatment on people with anorexia.[293]

People with anorexia repeatedly emphasize that a good relationship with a supportive clinician or clinical team is one of the most helpful and crucial aspects of treatment.[113] A positive therapeutic relationship requires empathy, trust, and a non-judgemental attitude, and is necessary for positive treatment outcomes. The development of the therapeutic alliance will be impeded if individuals with anorexia are viewed as untrustworthy[294-6] or if clinicians struggle to understand the complexities of anorexia. Brotman and colleagues[297] compared the reactions of doctors to anorexic, obese, and diabetic patients and found that anorexic patients provoked much greater stress and anger amongst doctors. They attributed this to doctors' perceptions of anorexia as "self-inflicted as opposed to biological." Ramjan[296] found that nurses had difficulties understanding the complexities of anorexia, and that a major source of stress and an obstacle to developing positive therapeutic relationships was "the struggle for control" when implementing programs to discipline people who were also seen as controlling.

### Challenges in working with parents and carers

Relationships between clinicians and parents or carers can also be fraught. Some parents and carers see clinicians as experts who will cure the person diagnosed with anorexia. Others have experienced clinicians who were unsupportive, unhelpful, lacked detailed knowledge about anorexia or the particular circumstances of individual families.[298] Tensions arise when parents and carers have unrealistic hopes, feel excluded from treatment decisions, or are unprepared for the financial and emotional burdens of anorexia and the possibility of unsuccessful intervention. Negative relationships between clinicians, parents, and carers can create an "us and them" relationship or trigger "doctor shopping," thereby impeding effective treatment and adding to the stress and anxiety of all involved.

## Challenges of working with other health professionals

Clinicians can struggle to ensure quality treatment if there are difficulties coordinating different health-care professionals or navigating the hierarchical relationships within treatment settings or between health-care professionals. These difficulties can be compounded if clinicians have different training, philosophies, or conceptualizations of anorexia or when insufficient specialist training means that problems are not identified until the well-being of the person with anorexia is compromised. Effective quality treatment can also be compromised if information is not shared, particularly as the person diagnosed with anorexia moves between different treatment phases.

## Self-care for clinicians

Clear and sensitive communication about the carer's expectations, the clinician's role and capacity to help, and the pooling of knowledge and information between health professionals is necessary from the onset. Given the complexity of anorexia, it is important for clinicians to work as part of a specialist, multidisciplinary team so there is a consistent approach to each case. Specific training for staff is also important and helpful, given the frustrations of working with people with anorexia. Clinicians need to practice self-care by sharing their frustrations and anxieties with colleagues and external supervisors, and by accessing additional support and knowledge when needed. Clinicians rely on parents and carers to ensure that people diagnosed with anorexia attend treatment and also to implement important treatment strategies at home. The challenges of working with teenagers with anorexia can be reduced if clinicians work with parents or carers to support recovery.

Over the next 12 months, Ruth's weight remained relatively stable but the anorexia did not release its hold. Ruth exercised religiously, directing her energy into competitive cross-country running. Her resistance to food also persisted and it was difficult to get her to eat. She'd tolerate a salad but anything else was a struggle. Ruth knew the nutritional content of every single item of food and refused "anything with an inkling of fat." Even when she went to a birthday party, Ruth insisted on taking her own meal of boiled rice. Beth found that her daughter's likes and dislikes changed the sort of meals she prepared for her family. On more than one occasion she caught herself out hiding the nutrition labels from food packets and calculating the calories and fat content of dishes so there wouldn't be a fuss at dinner.

When she started junior high school, Ruth found the transition difficult. None of her friends moved to the same school and Ruth was lonely. She moved between different friendship groups but couldn't find an accepting group that she slotted into comfortably. At the same time, Ruth wouldn't let anything interfere with her running training so it was hard to find the time to make new friends. As the school year inched forward, Ruth felt more and more like an outsider. She was often so miserable that she'd phone Beth during the school day for comfort and reassurance. In part as a distraction from the difficulties at school, Ruth increased her exercise regime—it was easy to forget her problems when she was running—but her body couldn't cope with the physical demands that she imposed on it. The weight just melted away, and by winter Ruth was so thin that she was constantly cold, cranky, and depressed.

Ruth was 14 years old when she was admitted to hospital for the second time. She resisted and protested, and spent days crying and complaining. Then it all changed. She was allowed out of hospital for two weeks to travel interstate with her class to compete in an interschool history quiz. Spending a fortnight with her classmates enabled her to see the girls in her class in a new light. They were a bright, bubbly bunch, always joking and having fun. Ruth couldn't resist being drawn into the fun. Her impish sense of humor made her popular company and she quickly formed the friendships she'd craved. The adventure opened Ruth's eyes to just *how* restricted her life had become, what a good time her new friends were having, and how much fun she was missing.

After the trip, Ruth returned to hospital with a new outlook. She and several other girls in the ward discovered that they had more in common than their eating disorder and became firm friends. Instead of being bored and spending her days doing little more than thinking about her anorexia, Ruth's mornings were busy with schoolwork and her afternoons were filled doing therapy and craft classes, chatting with the other girls,

---

**Box 8.3   Parents, Guilt, and Blame**

Parents, particularly mothers, feature in some theories about the causes of anorexia. This is consistent with a tradition in psychology of attributing a child's problems to his or her mother.[299–301] This view assumes that:

- the environment for children's development is synonymous with the mother because she is primarily responsible for child care[302]
- a good mother can produce a perfect, healthy, happy, and well-adjusted child.[303,304]

Less attention has been given to fathers in anorexia research and theory because they are historically considered to be less important in the development of children, especially girls.[305] When fathers are mentioned they are often portrayed as uninvolved and emotionally distant, critical, uncomfortable with their daughters' developing bodies, and as overvaluing achievement, perfectionism, and female attractiveness.[306,307]

Parent-blaming theories stigmatize parents, and they have not been proved by research.[64] They are often based on clinicians' observations of families at a time of extreme stress and anxiety,[64] and parents are more likely to behave in uncharacteristic ways if they feel patronized, stereotyped, blamed, or shamed.[149,308] Family problems identified as a cause of anorexia are just as likely to be the result of the presence of anorexia[9] and may also occur in "normal" families.[309] Parent blaming is increasingly regarded as unfair to parents and unhelpful for the treatment and recovery of individuals diagnosed with anorexia.[64]

---

watching movies, and trying out new make-up and hairstyles with her new friends. The friendships they established have continued and remained strong since Ruth returned home and the changed environment made her second hospital stay totally different to her first experience. It was a time when Ruth felt secure and "really safe."

With a different clinical team and a different attitude, Ruth found the nurses much friendlier and more approachable—they "didn't treat you like you were different or that you were really sly or something...a lot of them would talk to you and come into your room." Her new psychiatrist saw her several times a week and they had lengthy discussions about a multitude of issues, including her feelings, friends, school, and eating. He often stopped by just to say "Hi" when he visited the ward and Ruth felt he was genuinely interested in her well-being. Now that she was older and more confident, Ruth negotiated her treatment regime with the doctors and convinced them not to use nasogastric tube feeding but to give her a chance to put on weight by herself, simply by eating more food.

Looking back, Ruth believes the crucial turning point was making a conscious decision to recover. It suddenly hit her that she didn't really know who she was when she was sick: "I was just this person who just exercised and didn't eat all of the time." She could put on a front at school but it was draining and exhausting. In the familiarity of her own home, Ruth realized she was morose, irritable, and volatile. But her new friends and the different atmosphere in hospital gave her the tools to dig herself out of the dark hole she'd been trapped in:

> Something changed for me. I really wanted to get better. I stopped thinking I was fat. I don't know how that happened. I just felt like I really had to get better 'cause everyone else outside was really happy and I just couldn't do it myself so I just wanted to get better, I guess, and making friends with lots of people helped—it was more fun in there.

Beth and David were surprised and relieved that Ruth's second admission was so comparatively calm. They found the nurses "respectful and nice" and that Ruth's doctors willingly talked to Beth and David and involved them in working out the best ways to help Ruth move to recovery.

Ruth's anorexia impacted on everyone in the family. Her brother Callum was three years younger and accompanied Beth on the long drives to and from the hospital. This gave Beth the time to talk with Callum, to answer his questions, and to explore his feelings about his sister, but it ate into Callum's own time and his view of the world. David empathized:

> A couple of times he's said, "Is this [food] going to make me fat?" Just for a short period of time. I don't think it's bothering him too much now [but] basically Callum was feeling left out. Sometimes he would feel a little [and] look a bit down. He was okay playing PlayStation [at the hospital] for a little while but that gets boring. Even at home, there'd be a lot of arguments about "eat the food" or "don't eat the food" or "I'm not going to eat that" and so on. And he was there listening to it…he was only around about eight years old when it first happened and that's traumatic for a kid…you want to have no stress when you're that age. [When] everything's nice and peaceful at home, you feel good but when there are

stresses and anxiety and people yelling at each other, you feel uncomfortable.

For Beth, the main challenge has been coping with the distress. She felt the intensity of Ruth's suffering and was pained to see her bright, bubbly daughter turn into a shadow of her former self. Beth spent endless hours worrying and wondering about Ruth's well-being and future. At first, she also felt burdened by guilt and self-doubt that she might have unintentionally and unknowingly contributed to Ruth's problem in some way. Her feelings were eased when she met other parents at the hospital, got to know them and discovered that they were just "normal and nice" people.

---

**Box 8.4   Relationships between People with Anorexia**

People with anorexia often develop close relationships because they spend time together in hospital, recovery centers, and support groups, and communicate using the internet.

Relationships between people with anorexia can be negative if they compete to be the thinnest or the relationship reinforces or normalizes an identity as a person with anorexia or is a means for learning new weight-loss strategies like vomiting, exercising in secret, or artificially inflating weight for weigh-ins. Relationships between people with anorexia in hospital or treatment centers can have a negative impact if a gang mentality develops and people unite to sabotage treatment or to hide their transgressions of the treatment rules from the clinical staff.[136,137]

Relationships between people with anorexia can also be positive by providing a basis for discussing common concerns about food, exercise, relationships, and treatment and by providing consolation and sympathy during difficult times because of their shared understanding of the experience of anorexia.[85,310] People diagnosed with anorexia can also encourage and support each other in their efforts to recover and these positive relationships can help maintain recovery over the long term.

Like any other relationship, the complex interactions between individuals with anorexia can change over time. For instance, most people with anorexia find support groups helpful during the early stages of recovery, but support groups can delay latter stage recovery by maintaining a focus on the anorexia rather than allowing it to fade in importance.[119]

---

These encounters made her realize that there was no point in feeling guilty or distributing blame. Anorexia "can happen to the nicest families." Nevertheless, finding ways to keep herself "on an even emotional keel" was important to her own personal survival:

> You've got to do little things that make sure you enjoy life. It might be sitting and reading a book for half an hour with a cup of coffee. Having a bit of time out, if you need that. You know, little things, little moments in your life. You've got to have them. If I'm feeling too overloaded—and you can often feel that way when you're busy—it's good to take time out. Have a little nap, put a facial on, do your nails. Do something like that.

As a father, David worried about Ruth and the burdens her condition imposed on his family, especially for Beth who was at home "24 hours a day." As a doctor, Ruth's illness has challenged him to think about the coping strategies he would recommend to other parents confronting similar situations. He feels that sometimes parents need to insist on medical intervention—even if their child resists—but that once this critical stage has passed, parents can help their child make better lifestyle choices. It's crucial, he believes, for parents to communicate and work as a team with the clinicians because "one on one, a child will outmaneuver a parent every time."

Beth, David, and Ruth have different ideas about anorexia. David feels a person doesn't choose anorexia but it can be hard to give up because of "secondary gains" like additional attention. Beth feels, "You have to talk yourself out of thinking, 'Hey, you could stop this if you wanted to' [because] you know that they really can't. They can't control themselves. They can't stop it. It's like a mental illness." Ruth's own view lies somewhere in between:

> A lot of people think that it's your fault but it's not because you just can't control what you're thinking. I think it's probably the low self-esteem. You just want to change yourself, but you can't. You get scared that you're going to lose everything you've worked so hard for—all the dieting and exercising—if you start eating again so you just want to keep doing it...you can't just tell someone to eat. They're not going to do it and it's not their fault and it's not going to be easy and it takes like a long time to get better [but] you have to change how you think about yourself. No one else can do it for you. You have to make your own decision.

Ruth sees the changes in herself. She's now "busy enjoying herself" and has "heaps of friends." She's no longer "angry and grumpy" and "doesn't really care what other people think, as long as I'm healthy and happy with how I look." She's abandoned competitive running but doesn't think she'd turn back the clock even if she could. Ruth feels her illness has made her a different person—more understanding, independent, and determined: "It was a hard thing to get through but it just sort of makes you stronger."

Beth and David are delighted and relieved. Ruth's bright, funny personality has re-emerged and they love to see her making jokes, giggling with her girlfriends, and enjoying life. Yet they admit that Ruth is still a long way from being recovered. She's still "thinking about everything she puts in her mouth" and "not eating what you'd expect a normal teenage girl to eat," but they agree that life is more settled and peaceful and that, in many ways, the trauma of the last five years has brought the family closer together. With the support of a helpful counselor, Ruth has stayed on track for nearly six months and Beth and David are confident that they've finally seen the last of her anorexia and the eating disorders ward.

---

### Box 8.5   Supporting Parents

There is increasing recognition that parents can be valuable resources for helping a child with anorexia to recover.[129] Parents often need to encourage or compel a child to accept professional treatment[7] and parents' own emotional and behavioral responses to anorexia are also believed to influence treatment outcomes.[118,311]

Caring for a child with anorexia is a complex, demanding, and stressful role[146,147,219] and parents' interactions with health professionals can add to or help relieve the burden that parents experience.[148,202,312] Our interviews with parents of teenage girls with anorexia identified the types of support parents want from clinicians, health workers, and other professionals.

#### Including parents in treatment

- Parents want to be included in the clinical care of their child although the amount of involvement they desire varies.
- Parents want to be kept informed about their child's treatment and progress and to know what to expect next.

- Parents want clinicians to listen to their input and take it into consideration. Some parents also want the chance to give clinicians information without their child being present.

- Even though parents follow the recommendations of clinicians, they do not appreciate it when major decisions are made without consulting them or against their express wishes.

## Supporting and guiding parents in their daughters' care

As girls' primary carers but without professional training or experience with anorexia, parents appreciate the help and support of clinicians and other professionals, including:

- information about anorexia and its impact on families
- ideas about why their child might be behaving in certain ways
- advice about strategies to use at home including clear guidelines to follow and regular feedback on how they are doing
- clear rationales for recommended strategies
- advice and guidance that is tailored to their specific needs and circumstances and consistent with their values and beliefs
- post-discharge planning and follow-up
- personal coping strategies and positive ways of thinking about the illness
- counseling and emotional support
- opportunities to meet and develop supportive networks with other parents.

## Demonstrating positive attitudes toward parents

Parents appreciate professionals, services, and practices that demonstrate positive attitudes, including empathy, respect, and concern. While it may not always be possible to give parents everything they need or want, taking parents' perspectives into account enables clinicians to build productive and positive relationships with parents for the benefit of all concerned.

## Postscript

Beth has been in touch and left a message thanking us for writing the story and letting us know she thought what we'd written was "amazingly" accurate. Most importantly, she passed on the news that Ruth is now fully recovered.

# 9

# "It's All Up to Me Now"
## The Story of Renee, Elizabeth, Pat, and Ryan

Elizabeth and Pat have lived in the same rambling country house since they married more than 35 years ago. The house has aged gracefully. The spreading branches of the maple trees stretch out to tap on the windows, the shrubs edging the path to the house are a busy blaze of color, and the wide and welcoming porch is scattered with comfortable, well-worn chairs.

Elizabeth and Pat's early years together were marked by pain because their first child passed away just hours after being born. Elizabeth found release by talking to family, friends, and fellow church members but memories of the ordeal linger for both of them. Pat never had the opportunity to mourn and has been haunted by periodic bouts of depression ever since. Elizabeth remembers:

> I was patted on the back in the hospital and told you'll have plenty more babies. Thirty years ago when this happened, men weren't expected to grieve. They were expected to keep on going to work.

Despite the doctor's assurances, more babies didn't arrive. Elizabeth and Pat adopted a baby boy and called him Ryan. Seven years later, long after they'd given up hope of another child, Elizabeth became pregnant. It was a difficult pregnancy and Renee was premature and tiny, but her arrival brought joy to everyone in the family. She was a sweet, happy child doted on by her parents and adored by her older brother. Renee inherited her Irish grandmother's fiery spirit and her looks—curly red hair, green eyes, and the sort of skin that attracts more freckles than Renee would like.

Renee was 13 years old when Ryan left home to share a house with friends. Despite the difference in their ages, they were very close and Ryan's departure left a hole in Renee's life. She missed not having him around to chat with, confide in, and to tease her about her freckles. Elizabeth had been a stay-at-home mom until Renee became a teenager and she went back to work about the same time as Ryan moved out. Renee found the house eerily quiet. Elizabeth was no longer always on hand to chat and to keep Renee company whenever she wanted.

These were normal, everyday transitions but they coincided with a shift in Renee's eating behavior. She became more selective about the food she liked and disliked and more stubborn about what she'd eat and not eat. Elizabeth was a vegetarian so Renee's refusal to eat meat didn't cause alarm. Elizabeth and Pat were more concerned when Renee started refusing to eat *any* fat in *any* form, including cheese and other dairy products. However, they set aside their anxieties, reassuring themselves that this was just a temporary teenage phase—an isolated idiosyncrasy—that would soon right itself. But over the next 12 months, Renee progressively reduced the quantity and variety of foods she would eat until she was surviving on tiny salads that she'd linger over for hours. Renee became painfully thin and food became a battleground between mother and daughter. Elizabeth begged Renee to eat sensibly but her pleas only triggered tantrums and tears.

Convinced that malnutrition was at the heart of Renee's problems, Elizabeth asked Renee's teachers to monitor her eating at school. Renee was furious when she found out. She resented being put under surveillance but refused to concede that she was slowly starving herself to death. Elizabeth and Pat were distraught:

> We didn't know what to do. What *do* you do when your child's losing weight? We couldn't force her to eat. She was eating minute quantities of food. At school she wouldn't eat anything. She'd eat something really small for breakfast and then just drink water the whole day, and have a minute meal at night... Our family doctor really didn't know what to do either. (Elizabeth)

Renee's body was wasting away. She was always tired and irritable and suffered from constant circulation problems and painful chilblains on her fingers. The family doctor focused on these issues and referred her to a specialist to test her for lupus—an auto-immune disease that blocks the capillaries—but the seemingly endless litany of tests revealed nothing. By her fourteenth birthday, Renee's weight had dropped to only 29 kilos and, in spite of Renee's denials, the family doctor decided he was dealing with a case of anorexia nervosa. A fortnight before Christmas, Elizabeth and Pat took Renee to hospital on the pretence of having more lupus tests. Renee's anger was uncontainable when she found out she was being admitted to hospital for anorexia. Renee didn't believe the diagnosis and couldn't comprehend that she needed to alter her frugal eating behaviors. She blamed her mother and ranted and railed, accusing Elizabeth of betrayal and abusing her trust. Pat was relieved that Renee was finally being treated:

> Look, she wasn't getting any better. She just continued to deteriorate and she was getting so painfully thin that I was getting very worried…it wasn't really a shock to see her hospitalized considering the state she was in. I felt better that, you know, the matter had finally come to a head and was being addressed.

For Renee, hospital was a lonely, isolating experience. She was devastated to find herself in a stark hospital cubicle but she refused to decorate her cubicle with posters, photographs, flowers, and ornaments like the other girls on the ward. She was also much younger than the other girls and felt excluded from their intimate tête-à-têtes. Yet, at the same time, she didn't want to be involved when they clubbed together in defiance of the doctors' and nurses' directives. Renee's only goal was to get out of hospital. She ate everything she was offered and asked for more. Within a fortnight, she'd put on sufficient weight to be discharged. Looking back, Renee doesn't believe that being hospitalized had any lasting impact on her:

> I don't think [hospital] helps your state of mind because anorexia's such a long-term illness it can't possibly be treated in a short amount of time in hospital. And it doesn't help with learning to cope and build your life in the outside world. The hospital is a different environment. Your food is arranged on a tray and you're given the right proportions of things to eat and food supplements and all that sort of thing. So when you get out, you've still got no idea about how to cope in social situations with food when you're feeling really uncomfortable eating in front of people. I would just do anything to get out of [hospital] which was why I lied to myself that I was different to the other patients, that I didn't really have a problem, and that I could handle it on my own. So I put on weight just so that I could get out of there without really reflecting on why I was in there in the first place.

For the next two years, Renee's weight remained low but relatively stable. Nevertheless, troubling issues hid behind this façade. She was miserable, her self-esteem was low, she oscillated between self-starvation and overeating, and when she looked in the mirror all Renee saw was an overweight teenage girl staring back at her: "I might've looked alright on the outside but in my head I was still anorexic—I never really got back into a normal pattern of eating." Nor did Renee's preoccupation with food ease. Already an accomplished cook, Renee insisted on taking control of the organization and preparation of all the family's meals, and eliminated all sugar and fat from their diet. Pat didn't object. He'd been diagnosed with diabetes and Renee's dietary regime helped him stick to his prescribed diet. Besides, he rationalized, "She cooks very well [and] if she didn't cook what she likes to cook, she'd be in an even worse state of mind. She suffers from depression and she'd be far more depressed than she is."

Elizabeth had a different view and tried to encourage a more moderate approach. However, her efforts just incited anger and conflict. Tired of the constant tussles, Elizabeth decided that the only way to have peace and quiet was to hold her tongue. Pat agreed:

> Look, it's a compulsive disorder. They can't help what they're doing. It's as simple as that. You've just got to realize that there's no point in cajoling someone or being critical or anything like that because they're really not responsible for the way they're behaving. There's nothing that they can do about it. All you'd be doing is making them even unhappier than they already are… She gets cranky and—reactionary, I suppose, that would be the word? And you've got to ask yourself, "Are you really doing any good?" If you upset her, you're probably only going to make matters worse.

In her final year of school, Renee's eating disorder took a new turn for the worse that affected all aspects of her life:

> I began bingeing and purging pretty much every day. It was not only the physical effect on my body but the mental effect of not being able to concentrate on what it was I needed to concentrate on, and always having other thoughts going through my head concerning food and eating and what I was going to eat next. That *really* stopped me from achieving what I think I could have [at school] because my concentration was quite a bit lower.

After so many years of disciplined self-starvation, Renee took pleasure in over-indulging in the foods she'd denied herself, but her binges triggered feelings of guilt and self-loathing. In Renee's mind, purging was the only way to expel her feelings of revulsion towards herself. Renee admits that her bingeing and purging were more than a physical matter:

> It's a psychological thing as well. I feel I need to deny myself those things [I like to eat]. I can't let myself have them and I feel guilty if I do have them and I know this isn't normal. So it goes deeper than just wanting to eat some things and not wanting to put on weight…some foods are good and some are bad. So letting myself have those bad foods and really pigging out on them makes me a bad person. I feel like the word fat isn't just physical. For me, it incorporates laziness and greed and it's just all these things that I don't like rolled into one. That's the feeling that bingeing gives me. I need to get rid of those feelings and the only way I can do it is by making sure that I bring it all back up. I associate things like being greedy with being overweight. These ideas [have been] in my head from an early age—greed is bad and indulgence is bad. So eating a lot is greedy and self-indulgent and, therefore, bad.

Renee managed to hide her bingeing and purging from her parents for nearly 12 months but she felt guilty about being sly and deceptive. Just before her final school exams, Renee confessed to Elizabeth about her behavior. Renee felt release and relief that her secret was finally in the open but Elizabeth was engulfed by a whirl of conflicting emotions. She was shocked to learn of Renee's suffering and to discover that her beautiful daughter had such a painful, horrid problem. She was terrified of the implications for Renee's health and well-being and disappointed that she'd held off for so long before confiding in her and seeking her help. The confession made Elizabeth wonder if she could ever *really* know or understand exactly what Renee was experiencing. Elizabeth's main priority, however, was to keep the lines of communication open, but it was sometimes a struggle to find the balance between allowing Renee her privacy *and* some space to talk:

> Sometimes she'll say to me "I had a bad morning this morning"—meaning that she binged—but she doesn't really tell me much more than that and I don't probe too much unless I can see that she wants to talk to me about things because she's so sensitive. You know, that fine line can be crossed fairly easily.

## Box 9.1    The Meaning of Food

In today's society food means more than just satisfying hunger. The social meanings attached to food affect how we see ourselves, how we are viewed by others, and how we think and feel about food.

### Good and bad foods

Moral meanings are attached to the consumption of certain foods. Vegetables and fruit are seen as "good" foods because they are healthy, nourishing, and not fattening. People who choose "good" foods are regarded as self-disciplined and virtuous. Foods that are high in fat or sugar are considered "bad" foods and their consumption can be viewed as a sign of weakness or gluttony. In the same way, eating small or moderate portions of food denotes self-control while overeating suggests greed. Like lust, gluttony is a "sin of the flesh" and one of the seven deadly sins. People with anorexia are often seen as embodying the self-control and discipline over bodily desires that many people are unable to achieve.[313]

### Food as a comfort or reward

Foods are considered treats when they are sweet, expensive, time consuming to prepare, or used as rewards. For example, children may be given a lolly for being good or an adult may have a bottle of champagne to celebrate an achievement. People also eat particular foods when they feel depressed or tired. Chocolate and ice-cream are popular comfort foods because they are sweet and easy to eat.[277] Food is used to cope with emotional distress because it is easier to access and more socially acceptable than alcohol or drugs,[75] but many people with anorexia deprive themselves of food because they believe they do not deserve the pleasure it brings.[314]

### Food and femininity

In many societies, women are responsible for preparing food for their families yet are expected to restrain their own eating to maintain a slender body.[277] In such contexts, it is expected that women will eat smaller amounts of food than men and denying oneself food is regarded as an expression of culturally sanctioned feminine virtues and of self-sacrifice.[171]

osocial

Food +
Social
Class

### Food and social class

The sort of food eaten and the social practices around food reflect social standing, education, and income levels.[171] In western societies where high kilojoule food is abundant and inexpensive, eating this sort of food may be perceived as a sign of a lower socioeconomic status or class.[124] Being knowledgeable about food and nutrition and being selective about what one eats are markers of being well educated and prosperous.[128]

### Food and anorexia

The different ways in which individuals derive meaning from food are not merely cognitive. For people with anorexia, the meanings generated by food are an actual physical experience that forms an addictive, habitual pattern. It is the incorporation of these meanings into the body and mind and its impact on the whole person that make anorexia such a difficult problem to manage and to change.

Last week, Renee turned 18. She knows her physical, psychological, and social well-being has reached a critical point that can cause long-term problems. Renee has spent years on an emotional rollercoaster. She now takes antidepressants but their effectiveness is curtailed by the other chemical imbalances in her body. She hasn't menstruated for almost five years and this might make it difficult to conceive children. Her bone density and potassium levels are so low there is a strong risk of osteoporosis and she no longer has the energy to do the sort of things she enjoys doing:

> It has affected my stamina. I love walking and I often feel too tired to walk or go bike riding. I went for a bike ride with a few friends a couple of weeks ago and I was so buggered by the end of it, I just thought, "It'll be a long time before I can do that again." It really made me realize that if I want to do those sorts of things—things I *really enjoy* doing—I'm going to have to build myself up to do them because I've lost a lot of the stamina that I did once have.

Because she doesn't have the energy, plans for college have been put on hold. Renee also knows that her anorexia has reduced her independence and freedom:

My mother feels like it's her responsibility to look after me more than she would if I didn't have the problems with eating. I think my brother was a lot more independent than I am [at the same age]. Although I'm independent in some senses, I'm still emotionally dependent on them and I think that my mother sees it as her responsibility to care for me. It's the same for Dad in terms of keeping me and nurturing me.

Renee's hoping to try college again next year but, for the moment, she's taken a part-time job at a restaurant. Pat believes this has been a positive step:

Working has improved her self-esteem. You know, sort of given her something to get stuck into. She enjoys cooking enormously; it's a real love of her life. I think that's probably part of it but probably part of the condition so working in a restaurant, she's in her element.

Renee knows she still has "problems and conflicts in [her] mind about food and body image and self-esteem," but she's also seeing positive signs:

I'm feeling a lot more in control now than what I had been feeling; I guess my self-esteem is rising and I don't feel so down about myself. I still feel disappointed about not going to college and not doing more worthwhile things this year, but I'm able to sort of look over them now and think, oh well, I can pull myself out of this and think, well, next year it can be different.

Renee has spent a lot of time thinking about her anorexia and the particular form it has taken in her life. She has decided her eating problems have three dimensions. The physical dimension revolves around food and weight. This is the aspect of anorexia that attracts the greatest attention from family, the medical profession, the media, and the public. The emotional dimension of anorexia relates to her psychological well-being, self-esteem, and problem management. In hindsight, Renee wonders if her eating problems are a physical appeal for help for some deep, unidentified, inner distress. In Renee's schema, the spiritual dimension is the third and most important facet. This relates to the oneness between mind and body that seems to get lost when an eating disorder strikes. Renee feels that the fracturing of these three facets is at the heart of her illness. She's been so caught up in the physicality of her condition and in investing time and energy into monitoring her food, weight, and calories that she has lost contact with her spirituality and the "oneness" and peace that comes when mind and body work together in harmony. Renee believes that to recover she needs not only to banish the obsessions with food that make her miserable, but also to improve her self-esteem to enable the emotional growth necessary to regain a spiritual wholeness of body and mind.

Looking back on her personal history, particularly her experiences at school, Renee feels that neither the school curriculum nor school environment addressed key issues concerning eating disorders:

> In health and physical education classes there's a lot of discussion on being overweight, on obesity and the right way to eat and to cut down on fats. That's really drummed in. But there's not a lot about eating disorders or about mental health. There's not a lot about feeling good about yourself and I think [anorexia is about] how you feel about yourself. I think school should [focus on] self-confidence and how you feel about your body, your body image, and self-perception. I think all the eating disorders—even overeating and compulsive eating—are based on the same logic in your head. They're all to do with a friction between your mind and your body and not being able to handle things [and] deal with emotions.

Renee's reflection on her anorexia has stimulated her interest in how social attitudes and the media influence girls' self-esteem and need to control food. Renee doesn't believe the media causes or is to blame for anorexia amongst teenage girls but she does believe it presents an idealized notion of body, appearance, and femininity that feeds into the collective subconscious in ways that pressure women to desire and strive for a fantasized ideal of beauty. Renee is frustrated and annoyed by the attitudes to anorexia she's encountered in the media and wider society:

> Society as a whole doesn't have a lot of information about eating disorders. It's up there with a lot of the mental illnesses [and] a lot of psychiatric problems that aren't discussed very openly. Superficial assumptions are made that it's a disorder brought on yourself because you want to look a certain way. People don't understand that there are a lot of psychiatric problems behind it. The stigma is about the superficiality of this disease.
>
> I think that an eating disorder is a lot deeper than looking at a magazine cover and thinking I want to look like her…if you talk to an anorexic person, there's no way they're going to assume that they will look like a supermodel if they develop anorexia. It's never an intention to

do that. It's a lot more to do with self-esteem and emotional problems and the way they deal with them than it is with the actual physical presentation of anorexia.

On an intellectual level, Renee knows her body will stop functioning if she continues to starve herself and to binge and purge. At an emotional level, though, she is terrified of gaining weight and panics with each small increase on the bathroom scales. Reflecting on her illness has helped Renee understand herself and how her eating disorder has become entangled

---

## Box 9.2   Religion and Spirituality

Historically, self-starvation has been associated with gender. Christian women starved themselves to demonstrate their piety, as penance for their sins or a strategy to be closer to God.[18] In contrast, men were more likely to demonstrate piety by relinquishing their power, money, or prestige. The religious connotations attached to self-starvation have persisted in the contemporary language of people who describe their eating disorder in religious and moral terms, for example, by describing weight gain as evil and a lower weight as bringing them closer to God.[315]

Lelwica[313] argues that in modern western societies, the distinction between the sacred (traditional religions) and secular (media images) has been blurred and that a decrease in conventional religious practices has led women to seek answers to life's problems in popular culture. She argues that images of thin models serve a function similar to that of holy persons and saints by presenting an ideal to aspire to. Rituals like dieting have a purifying function akin to confession or atonement for one's sins.

Some writers suggest the faith of religious individuals diminishes as their anorexia becomes more prominent but increases in recovery.[316,317] Others argue that spiritual healing is important in recovery[318] and can provide individuals with meaning and help reintegrate the body and the mind if these were previously at odds with each other.[113]

While anorexia can be considered to be a way of responding to the difficulties of life, spiritual healing involves finding and creating *alternative spiritual resources*—images, rituals, beliefs, communal connections, and moral sensibilities—that enable individuals to address the disappointments of life in positive, transformative ways. Spiritual healing is an ongoing process of self-transformation and growth that involves finding ways to move beyond an existence driven by the narrow goal of getting or staying thin to a larger, more substantive and meaningful life.

with her identity. Her reflection has also opened up a path to recovery. It has helped to identify the attributes she doesn't want to be part of her identity any longer: the self-criticism that has demolished her self-esteem; the desperate need to control food preparation at all times; the emotional strain and social difficulties which her anxieties about food and eating create.

Until recently, Renee kept her traumatic relationship with food a secret from everyone but her parents. She worried about being dismissed as superficial, vying for attention, wanting to look like a supermodel or believing that "losing weight will make my life perfect." When she finally plucked up the courage to tell her friends, she found they were supportive but also a source of additional anxiety and guilt:

> They really want to help me and there's nothing they can do. So that makes me feel even worse because I know that now I've upset them [and] they are aware that I'm upset but there's nothing they can do to make me feel better.

Four years after her initial diagnosis, Renee recognizes that she's had a problem for a long time. At first, she thought she could deal with it herself and that all she had to do was flick "a magic switch" and she'd recover. She now knows that much more is involved. Renee won't contemplate being admitted to hospital again but she's taken the initiative by seeing a doctor and social worker as an outpatient at the local hospital:

> At the time, I felt that perhaps once I'd said it aloud, the problem would go away and that by saying that I had a problem it would somehow make it disappear. When it became obvious that that wasn't how it was going to happen, I soon realized that I was going to need some kind of other help... Once the doctor actually said, "You know you *do* have a problem and there's something you have to do," it made it more concrete. I saw it as officially "a problem" and a big problem.

The doctor is caring for Renee's physical well-being and the social worker is helping her deal with the psychological adjustments needed to recover. Renee finds it hard to admit to others that she's seeing a doctor and social worker but she concedes that they are helping her. Renee is feeling happier, physically better, and more emotionally in control. Pat has noticed the improvement in her eating:

I think things have settled down and are still going on fairly normally in terms of her condition. I mean, she is eating reasonably well. She eats reasonable sized meals and she's not eating, you know, just lettuce or having the preoccupation with salad like she used to have. She eats a lot of different kinds of vegetables and protein, you know, different kind of beans and what have you. I think there probably could be some more protein in her diet, but it's certainly not as deficient as it used to be when she was younger.

---

## Box 9.3  Media and Anorexia

Representations of anorexia in newspapers, talk shows, current affairs programs, documentaries, and women's magazines fall into three broad categories. The first category comprises "narratives of the macabre." These media stories seek to shock the public with graphic photos of emaciated bodies and by dwelling on how little individuals eat and weigh or on unusual behaviors and attitudes. Such stories sensationalize anorexia as a spectacle and present people with anorexia as incomprehensible or grotesque. Illustrative is the international coverage of singer Karen Carpenter's anorexia and death.[319]

The second category of media coverage comprises "info-docs" that aim to provide the public with an accurate, realistic understanding of the complexity of anorexia and its impact. Typical are documentaries and current affairs programs that present factual information and real-life experiences of people with anorexia and their families in a sensitive, rather than sensationalized, way.[320,321]

The third category of media coverage consists of "narratives of recovery and cure." These feature stories of recovery and accounts of "successful" recovery treatments. Some stories report on scientific and medical advances in treatment. Others ignore the scientific evidence by presenting a new treatment as a miracle cure and have triggered expressions of concern from clinicians and others that "narratives of recovery and cure" may encourage individuals and families to pin their hopes on expensive, unproven, or potentially dangerous recovery strategies.[322,323]

Media portrayals of anorexia can shape popular ideas and beliefs about anorexia and how the general public responds to people with anorexia and their families.[324] This can be a cause of frustration for people with anorexia.[325] Media stories that portray celebrities with anorexia as glamorous, romantic figures promote an image of anorexia as a foible of the rich and spoilt and feed public perceptions that anorexia results from a desire to be thin and beautiful, and to emulate media celebrities.[325,326]

Television programs, popular magazines, and advertising are often accused of contributing to eating disorders by presenting thinness as essential to female beauty and desirable for the successful woman, thereby increasing the pressure on women to strive for an idealized notion of womanhood. As Smolak[327] describes: "The dominant feminine role modeled for today's girls and college women is the superwoman... women should be able to 'have it all': good career, happy marriage, healthy children, an active social life and good looks."

Research reveals that media images and stories do not cause anorexia but they do create a cultural climate in which the self-starving behavior of girls and women is rewarded, encouraged, admired, and praised. For individuals who lack some larger purpose in life, the project of self-starvation and being thin can become all consuming. There is some evidence of a positive relationship between exposure to thin women in the media and women's dissatisfaction with their bodies and disordered eating. While this does not necessarily translate into anorexia, it may play a role in shaping the social pressures and perceptions of beauty and success that are prevalent in contemporary society.[186]

While definitive scientific explanations of the relationship between media and anorexia are elusive, social analysts argue that the idealization of thinness as integral to beauty and womanly perfection is socially undesirable because it teaches women to measure their worth and value according to the size of their bodies. Consequently, media critique is often considered a central component of prevention, education, and treatment programs for anorexia because it teaches girls and women to reorientate their thinking from criticizing their bodies to critiquing the culture that encourages and supports self-destructive eating behaviors.[313]

Nevertheless, Renee is frustrated that her recovery seems so slow. She keeps asking herself, "Shouldn't I be better by now?" The doctor and social worker have helped her understand "that getting better does not happen simply by deciding to get well but that it takes a long time." Recovery is a journey.

Despite Renee's resolve to recover, Elizabeth and Pat are worn down by the trauma and heartache of struggling to try and stop Renee from slipping away from them: "There's tension all the time, so you're angry with each other. Everybody's angry." Elizabeth's feelings about Renee's eating problems are so turbulent that she struggles to put them into words—anger, frustration, sadness, distress. Mostly, it's a sense of guilt:

> It's the exact feeling that I had when our first child died. It must have been something I did. You think that for years when you're grieving—it's something that I did. You just keep blaming yourself and going over and over it and thinking, "If I hadn't done that it would be alright." It's stupid but you can't stop it. It's the guilt, I suppose. You feel ashamed [because it's] so tragic. That's exactly how I feel about Renee's eating disorder. I feel ashamed because I feel it's probably got something to do with something I've done. I feel responsible because I'm her mother... I should have known or stopped it happening way back. I can't really express it. It's like I've failed.

---

### Box 9.4   Readiness for Recovery

Why do people diagnosed with anorexia seem to resist recovery even though anorexia causes them so much distress? Anorexia can serve different functions for different people. It can forestall the process of growing up and becoming independent or sexually mature. It may give a sense of competence, self-control, and moral purity that an individual fears might otherwise be lacking. It may seem to make life simpler and more predictable or protect an individual from having to think about more painful issues. Sometimes anorexia is so entangled with a person's identity that it is inconceivable to be without it. At the same time, starvation and depression can also inhibit the capacity to think rationally or contemplate a different way of life.[175]

Researchers, clinicians, people diagnosed with anorexia, and those who have recovered are in agreement that recovery often depends on motivation and readiness to change.[85,328] People may reach a critical point of readiness at different times and in very individual ways. Some people have identified positive life events as key events on the road to their recovery, for example: rewarding work or education; becoming pregnant and having children; removing themselves from destructive relationships and environments. Others have said that they had simply matured, realized the emotional and physical cost of their anorexia, or wanted a better life.

Theoretical models that explain how people go about changing addictive behaviors such as drinking and gambling have been used to understand eating disorders. For example, the Stages of Change model identifies six stages in the progression of anorexia:[329–31]

- *precontemplation*: the person is not aware of the problem or has no intention of doing anything about it
- *contemplation*: the person is willing to consider but will not commit to change
- *preparation*: the person is committed to changing in the near future
- *action*: the person is actively working toward change
- *maintenance*: the person is working to sustain the improvements made
- *termination*: the person is no longer tempted to relapse into the old behaviors.

In the Stages of Change model, as in similar models, the motivation to change depends on a person's view of the desirability or importance of the change and their capacity to change.[328,332]

Some experts disagree with the idea of stages of change and believe that change is a continuous process.[333] Others have argued that anorexia is more complex than other addictive behaviors because it involves changing multiple behaviors such as food restriction, bingeing, purging, and over-exercising.[334] Furthermore, a person with anorexia may feel motivated to discard symptoms of anorexia that have a negative effect on well-being, such as preoccupation with food, physical illness, low mood, and difficulty with relationships.[328,335] Yet they may be unwilling to relinquish aspects of their anorexia that they value, such as low weight and rigid control of food.[175] Even people who are taking positive action to change report feeling ambivalent about recovery if they see anorexia as both a friend and an enemy.[85]

Regardless of the disagreement about whether particular models of change should be used to guide treatment, there is consensus that increasing a person's motivation to change is important.[331,334,336] One treatment strategy that is used to try to move individuals towards change is Motivational Interviewing.[337] This is a style of counseling in which series of questions are used to help the individual explore and understand their ambivalence to recovery. Because confrontation is thought to increase resistance, this approach uses a warm, collaborative, and empathetic style designed to reduce the negativity of individuals diagnosed with anorexia.[332]

While the desire to recover is important, exactly how this motivation comes about is often a mystery, not only for clinicians and researchers but also for people with anorexia.

Sometimes, the relentlessness of coping grinds Elizabeth down and she gets angry at the world. When these feelings take hold, she avoids Renee. Elizabeth knows that it's the illness, not Renee, that is the cause of her anger. She's been annoyed by the lack of professional support for parents in her district but has been comforted by her friends and her faith. When life gets so difficult that she can't see a way forward Elizabeth repeats one of her favorite prayers: "All things change, only God remains."

Pat admires Elizabeth's patience and is grateful to her. Not only has Elizabeth borne the brunt of Renee's eating problems, but she has done so while looking after her aging mother who lives with the family for most of each year. Pat's work for local charities has kept him busy and distracted but he's also been preoccupied with his own physical and emotional difficulties:

> I've been struggling with alcohol for several years. I'm perfectly alright at the moment but I do suffer terrible depression at times. I really get very, very depressed. I've gone through a fairly bad bout of depression, partly I suspect because I'm one of these people that gets depressed through the winter months. In the last few weeks, I'm starting to feel really good. And the other thing is that I was diagnosed as being diabetic about three or four years ago. I've gone on to a much stronger medication in the last fortnight and I'm starting to feel better than I've felt in the last 12 months. It's really much, much better. My thinking is a lot clearer and I'm feeling a lot calmer too. Anyway, I'm certainly feeling much more positive.

Elizabeth and Pat feel Renee's lucid reflection on her illness is a significant shift in her thinking and attitudes. They're relieved by this change and believe it's important for her recovery but they're wary of being seduced into being prematurely hopeful. They see recovery as a promise for the future rather than a reality in the present. They feel that Renee, at 18 years of age, is no longer a child and that she has to rise to the task of taking responsibility for her own physical and emotional well-being. Renee agrees:

> It's all up to me now. I know logically what I need to do, it's just the matter of doing it that I find so difficult.

# 10

# Conclusion

The family biographies in *Inside Anorexia* illuminate the diverse forms that anorexia can take. While popular opinion tends to view anorexia simply as self-starvation—deliberately depriving oneself of food—the stories in *Inside Anorexia* reveal that anorexia is *much* more complex. The eating behaviors of people diagnosed with anorexia are very different and often change over time. Anorexia also involves more than controlling the *consumption* of food. It often involves complex rituals around the *preparation* of food. Hannah, for instance, imposed rigid routines on preparing the carrots and vegetables she ate for dinner and on *how* she ate her food. Jo had different but equally rigid rituals about the order in which she ate different foods. In many instances, people with anorexia extend their urge to control food to controlling the food of other family members. Kate and Renee, for instance, insisted on taking charge of the kitchen and cooked copious quantities of food for their families. Ruth used her knowledge of the fat and calorie content of foods to monitor and discipline her mother's preparation of meals.

The family biographies also reveal that anorexia involves much more than food. Parents and girls described the intense passions that can operate in concert with the push for thinness: the drive to achieve at school, in sport, at dance, at being the "best anorexic;" the compulsion to exercise in spite of its negative effects on girls' bodies, emotional well-being, or family and social relations. In some cases, more extreme and tragic behaviors can be part of the experience of anorexia. Kate was held captive by an obsessive-compulsive need to count and to clean, while Jo's anorexia was accompanied by self-destructive self-mutilation and suicide attempts. For all the girls whose stories are presented here, the development of anorexia brought significant changes in their behavior and their physical and

emotional capacity to participate in the sort of activities and social relations that generally fill a teenager's life.

The stories in this collection also reveal that anorexia is not a static
entity. Its form and expression can change over time. This quality makes
anorexia an especially challenging condition for parents, siblings, friends,
and others. For example, Renee recounted how her eating behaviors
shifted from self-starvation to daily bingeing and purging. Ruth, Hannah,
Carol, and Antonia all described experiencing a metamorphosis from
"normal" dieting to a radical reduction in the range and quantity of foods
they ate. Such shifts are always accompanied by the emergence of new
behaviors and different physical and psychological issues that present a
fresh set of challenges for those diagnosed with anorexia, their parents and
families, and for the clinicians and other professionals who are working to
support them.

Despite this diversity, several common threads are woven through the
girls' and parents' accounts of living with anorexia. Three of these warrant
particular comment because they were especially significant for the girls
and parents whose stories are recounted in *Inside Anorexia* and because they
echo the patterns identified by other researchers, clinicians, and eating disorders experts amongst people diagnosed with anorexia and their families
in general.

The first of these threads is the deep entanglement of anorexia in the
individual experiences, environments, and sociocultural circumstances of
each person's life. Experiences that the girls identified as especially significant included intense social pressure to be thin that manifested itself in
hurtful comments about their body shape or weight by peers or others
(Carol, Kate, Antonia, Jo) and that led them to desire the same physical
shape they believed other girls had (Hannah), or that was prevalent in particular social cultures where thinness was viewed as desirable or necessary
to excel, such as ballet, dancing, and sport. In hindsight, Carol, Ruth,
Angela, and Hannah all believed that the pressures to be thin experienced
in their particular sociocultural environments and circumstances increased
their vulnerability to self-destructive eating and exercising patterns.

It is important to note that these are illustrative instances. There is wide
variation in the particular sociocultural contexts in which anyone diagnosed with anorexia is located. Nevertheless, the girls and their parents
recognized the impact of such influences and their views echo a growing

body of research that has illuminated the subtle but significant ways in which different sociocultural environments and contexts can nurture disordered eating and behaviors, as is evident in our discussions of the role of the media, schooling, and the messages imbedded in the ideology of healthism.[2,163,183]

The second thread woven through the family biographies is the impact of girls' self-esteem and feelings about their bodies on their lives. Carol, Renee, and Kate, for instance, describe the detrimental effects of their feelings about themselves and their bodies: how it eroded their self-confidence; made them withdraw from social interaction; and played into the development and maintenance of their anorexia. Such personal experiences reverberate with an extensive body of research that documents the connection between self-esteem, anorexia, and its accompanying problems.[35] Underlining this connection, girls like Carol and Angela testified that improving their self-esteem was an important move towards recovery.

The third strand that is evident in the family biographies is the intricate entanglement of anorexia with girls' sense of personal identity and purpose. It was Kate who made this point explicit when she said, "If you're not the girl with anorexia, then who are you?" For most people, anorexia becomes much more than just a condition or an illness. It becomes a way of life and a way of defining oneself. At least in part, the enmeshment of anorexia with a person's sense of self helps explain the difficulty and trauma involved in recovery because it requires individuals to relinquish a way of being that circumscribes how they see and know themselves.[313,318]

Perhaps the most striking feature of the family biographies in *Inside Anorexia* is that they reveal how little escapes anorexia's effects. Anorexia permeates the minutiae of daily life in ways that affect everyone in a family: stress levels increase; daily routines like meals, shopping, school, and work change; time and energy are directed from other activities to seeing clinicians or visiting the hospital; relations between family members alter; and the family's plans, hopes, and expectations for the future often need to be amended and revised.

For most parents, the presence of anorexia in the family is a test of resilience, devotion, and the ability to adapt to the changes that occur during the illness. Parents find themselves constantly questioning, searching for answers, and engaging in a perpetual process of experimentation to find the strategy, approach, or clinician that seems to work with their child at a particular point in time. As the stories shared by parents reveal, this process can involve disappointment and heartache. But this is not always the case. Kate's parents discovered that family therapy gave them the confidence and strategies to manage Kate and to make family life more harmonious and workable. Hannah's parents, after many forlorn attempts, finally found a doctor who could manage their daughter and, as a result of their own research, discovered that treating Hannah and her anorexia as different personalities enabled them to help Hannah move towards recovery. For parents and families, living with anorexia involves a learning cycle. In broad terms, this process consists of three phases:

1.   *An accumulating knowledge phase* that involves ferreting out information from a range of sources to get a better understanding of anorexia, its implications and effects, and different management strategies and ways of helping individuals move towards recovery. During this learning phase, parents and families access a wide range of information sources. These include the expertise of physicians, clinicians, and other health professionals but also popular literature, academic publications, the internet, and formal and informal networks that include family members, friends, work colleagues, and eating disorders support groups.

2.   *An assimilation phase* when new knowledge and different perspectives are weighed up, evaluated, and either adopted or excluded based on parents' knowledge of their child or the specific circumstances of each family. Invariably, this phase involves making decisions on issues and aspects of anorexia where eating disorders experts hold different views or perspectives, many of which are summarized throughout *Inside Anorexia*.

3.   *A decision-making phase* when parents use the knowledge they have acquired to make choices about future action. Sometimes this involves questioning the opinion of experts. This can be a difficult step, as Antonia's mother learned when she queried her daughter's diagnosis. Yet bringing together parents' real-life knowledge of their child and the professional

expertise of clinicians can be a potent formula for positive change and improvement, as Kate's parents discovered when they collaborated with their family therapy counselor.

Because anorexia is not a stable entity, these three learning phases are repeated—to a greater or lesser degree—as an individual's condition or circumstances change, although the work involved in each phase diminishes as knowledge is accumulated.

*Inside Anorexia* illustrates the diversity, complexity, and challenges that anorexia presents for girls, parents and families, clinicians, as well as for the growing number of professionals, such as teachers, counselors, social workers, and health workers, who deal with anorexia on a daily basis. Such diversity is a reminder that the experience of anorexia is different for everyone and that a one-size-fits-all approach is insufficient for managing such a complex condition. Rather, *Inside Anorexia* demonstrates that the starting point for understanding anorexia must be the unique stories and experiences of individuals and their families.

While energetic, high-quality research continues to be conducted in the hope of finding definitive answers, *Inside Anorexia* illustrates that experts from different disciplines currently have different perspectives on aspects of anorexia. This should be seen as a help rather than a hindrance. Such varied insights provide the range of knowledge and resources necessary when tackling a problem as diverse and complex as anorexia, particularly amongst the most vulnerable group of people with anorexia nervosa: teenage girls.

# International Advisory Panel

**Neil W. Boris, MD**, is an Associate Professor in the Department of Community Health Sciences at the Tulane University School of Public Health and Tropical Medicine in New Orleans, Louisiana, USA. He trained as a pediatrician and child and adolescent psychiatrist in keeping with his passion for promoting the health and mental health of children at risk. Since completing his medical residency, he has had consistent research funding from 12 separate agencies or foundations, has co-authored more than 40 peer-reviewed publications and another 30 chapters in leading textbooks of pediatrics and psychiatry. A significant focus of Dr Boris' research has been on the social and emotional development of young children in high risk environments and he has been the Principal Investigator on three major longitudinal studies examining interventions involving at risk and socioeconomically disadvantaged children. Dr Boris is on the editorial boards of two major international journals and the board of directors of local and international child-focused professional organizations. He has had international teaching appointments and his current research involves evaluating interventions for orphaned children in Africa.

**Simon Clarke, MB BS**, is Head of the Department of Adolescent Medicine at Westmead Hospital and the Director of Adolescent Medicine for Sydney West Area Health Service in Sydney, Australia. As a pediatrician and adolescent physician, he is one of Australia's pioneers in adolescent health and well-being. Dr Clarke opened Australia's first hospital adolescent ward in May 1983. As well as managing other cases, the adolescent unit at Westmead Hospital specializes in the management of children and adolescents with eating disorders. In addition to his clinical interests, much of Dr Clarke's scientific research and publications have focused on the area of eating disorders. This work includes studies of the genetics of anorexia nervosa, body composition in untreated and treated anorexia nervosa patients, nasogastric feeding, and parents' and siblings' reactions to patients with anorexia. Dr Clarke is currently involved in a study examining the effects of starvation on brain and mood changes before and after refeeding.

**John Evans, BEd (Hons), MA, PhD**, is Professor of Sociology of Education and Physical Education in the School of Sport and Exercise Sciences, Loughborough University, England. His publications include: *PE, Sport and Schooling: Studies in the Sociology of PE* (Falmer Press, 1986); *Teachers, Teaching and Control* (Falmer Press, 1988); *Equality, Education and Physical Education* (Falmer Press, 1993); *Politics, Policy and Practice in Physical Education* (with F. Dawn Penney and F.H. Spon, 1999); *Knowledge and Control: Studies in the Sociology of Physical Education and Health* (Routledge, 2004); and *Educational Policy and Social Reproduction* (with John Fitz and Brian Davies, Routledge, 2005). He is editor of a special edition of *The Curriculum Journal*, "International Perspectives on Physical Education," and founding editor of the international journal *Sport, Education and Society*. He has published widely in the sociology of education and physical education. His current research with Dr Emma Rich centers on the relationships between obesity discourses, formal education, and the development of eating disorders. He is leading, with Dr Emma Rich, an investigation into "The Impact of Health Imperatives on Schools" that has been funded by the UK's Economic and Social Research Council.

**Daniel le Grange, BA, BA (Hons), MA, PhD**, is Associate Professor of Psychiatry in the Department of Psychiatry, Section for Child and Adolescent Psychiatry, and Director of the Eating Disorders Program at the University of Chicago. He received his doctoral education at the Institute of Psychiatry, University of London, and trained in family-based treatment for adolescent anorexia nervosa at the Maudsley Hospital in London where he was a member of the team that developed the "Maudsley Approach" as a treatment for early onset anorexia nervosa. He completed a postdoctoral fellowship at the Maudsley Hospital, University of London and introduced the "Maudsley Approach" to his colleagues when he moved to the United States to do a postdoctoral fellowship at Stanford University. Dr le Grange is the author or co-author of more than 100 research and clinical articles, abstracts, books, and book chapters. Most of his scholarly work is in the area of family-based treatment for adolescent eating disorders and includes the first study of two outpatient family-based treatments for adolescents with anorexia nervosa. With Lock, Agras and Dare, Dr Grange is author of the *Treatment Manual for Anorexia Nervosa: A Family-based Approach* (Guilford Press, 2001) and co-author (with James Lock) of *Help your Teenager Beat an Eating Disorder* (Guilford Press, 2005) and *Treating Bulimia in Adolescents: A Family-based Approach* (Guilford Press, 2007).

**Michael Kohn, MB BS**, is a pediatrician and a clinical researcher specializing in treatment outcomes and eating, behavioral, and learning disorders.

After completing pediatric training in Sydney, Australia, Dr Kohn completed a Fellowship in Adolescent Medicine at the Albert Einstein College of Medicine in New York. Since returning to Australia in 1996 he has continued clinical and research interests at The Children's Hospital at Westmead in Sydney, Australia where he is presently a Senior Staff Specialist and a Senior Clinical Lecturer in the Faculty of Medicine at Sydney University. Dr Kohn's main research interest has been investigating aspects of nutrition and neuroscience, particularly amongst teenagers with eating disorders. In collaboration with an active clinical research team at the Westmead Campus, he has published more than 50 peer-reviewed scientific articles and five book chapters. He is currently investigating the effects of Strattera.

**Michelle Lelwica, MTS, PhD**, is the author of *Starving for Salvation: The Spiritual Dimensions of Eating Problems among American Girls and Women* (Oxford University Press, 1999) based on her doctorate research at Harvard University. Her most recent book, *The Religion of Thinness* (Gürze Press, 2008), is written for a popular audience and examines the spiritual dimensions of body image and eating problems. Dr Lelwica received her doctorate from Harvard Divinity School in the area of Religion, Gender and Culture in 1996 and received her Masters of Theological Studies from Harvard Divinity School in the area of Christianity and Culture in 1989. Dr Lelwica has published scholarly articles on religion and women's conflicted relationship to food and their bodies and has lectured widely on the topic. Her current research focuses on the dynamics and effects of the globalization of the Euro-American ideal of female thinness to women in postcolonial contexts. Dr Lelwica teaches courses dealing with Religion and the Body, Women and Religion, and Religion and Culture in the Religion Department and the Women's Studies Program at Concordia College in Moorhead, Minnesota, USA.

**James Lock, MD, PhD**, is Professor of Child Psychiatry and Pediatrics in the Department of Psychiatry and Behavioral Sciences at Stanford University School of Medicine, where he also serves as Director of the Eating Disorder Program for Children and Adolescents. His major research and clinical interests are in psychotherapy research, especially in children and adolescents, and specifically for those with eating disorders. Dr Lock has published more than 150 articles, abstracts, and book chapters. He is the author, along with le Grange, Agras and Dare, of the *Treatment Manual for Anorexia Nervosa: A Family-based Approach* (Guilford Press, 2001). He is co-author (with le Grange) of a book for parents called *Help your Teenager Beat an Eating Disorder* (Guilford Press, 2005) and a treatment manual for adolescent bulimia nervosa entitled *Treating Bulimia in Adolescents: A Family-based Approach* (Guilford Press, 2007).

Dr Lock is the recipient of a Career Development Award and a Mid-Career Award, both funded by the National Institute of Mental Health in the United States and focused on enhancing psychosocial treatments of eating disorders in children and adolescents. He is the principal investigator at Stanford on a multi-site trial comparing individual and family approaches to anorexia nervosa in adolescents, funded by the United States' National Institute of Health.

**Sloane Madden, MB BS (Hons), CAPCert**, is a child and adolescent psychiatrist at The Children's Hospital, Westmead in Sydney, Australia. His special interests are eating disorders, neuroimaging and neuropsychiatry. He is Deputy Head of the Department of Psychological Medicine and manages the hospital's eating disorder program in conjunction with adolescent physician Dr Michael Kohn. He is a member of the 2006, 2008 and 2009 International Academy of Eating Disorders Conference Scientific and Organizing Committee and has recently had articles published on his research on family therapy in eating disorders, the use of nasogastric feeding in eating disorders, and the role of siblings in eating disorders.

**Emma Rich, BSc (Hons), PhD**, is a lecturer in Physical Education, Gender, Identity and Health in the School of Sport and Exercise Sciences at Loughborough University, England. Her research interests include: gender and physical education/sport; the social construction of (ill) health; processes of medicalization; equity, inclusion, and identity in physical education; and health and cyberspace. She has published journal articles and books on sociology, education, physical education, sociology of health and illness, and feminist studies. Her work with Professor John Evans and Rachel Allwood exploring the relationship between education, eating disorders, and the obesity epidemic has been published internationally in the sociology of education, physical education and health communities, and has received growing attention from international media. Dr Rich is co-author of the forthcoming books with Routledge, *Medicalisation of Cyberspace* (with Andy Miah) and *Fat Fabrications* (with John Evans) and is the founder of the International Gender, Sport and Society Forum. She is co-investigator with John Evans on "The Impact of Health Imperatives on Schools", a research project funded by the Economic and Social Sciences Research Council in the United Kingdom.

**Stephen Touyz, BSc, BSc (Hons), PhD**, is Professor of Clinical Psychology at the University of Sydney and holds an honorary Chair in the Department of Psychological Medicine (Psychiatry). He is Co-Director of the Peter Beumont Centre for Eating Disorders at Wesley Private Hospital and a consultant to the

Eating Disorders Program at Westmead Hospital in Sydney, Australia. Professor Touyz is the immediate past president of the Eating Disorders Research Society and is an executive member of both the Australian and New Zealand Academy of Eating Disorders and the Eating Disorders Foundation. Professor Touyz has written and/or co-authored five books and has published more than 170 articles and book chapters. Professor Touyz is currently the leading investigator on two large research projects funded by the National Health and Medical Research Council in Australia on the treatment of anorexia nervosa.

# About the Authors

**Associate Professor Christine Halse, BA (Hons) Dip Ed, PhD**, is Chief Investigator of the multidisciplinary, multi-method Australian Research Council project Multiple Perspectives of Eating Disorders in Girls at the University of Western Sydney, Australia. She has published widely on anorexia nervosa, particularly on biographical issues, cross-disciplinary perspectives of clinical problems and the ethical issues involved in working with teenage girls with anorexia. Dr Halse is internationally regarded as a biographer and for her work on the impact of life history on practical problems. She is the author of *A Terribly Wild Man: The Life of the Reverend Ernest Gribble* (Allen & Unwin, 2002), the story of the most famous and infamous missionary to the Australian Aborigines.

**Dr Anne Honey, BEc, B Applied Science (Occ Therapy) (Hons), PhD**, has a background in mental health research and occupational therapy. She is the Senior Researcher with the Multiple Perspectives of Eating Disorders in Girls project at the University of Western Sydney, Australia. Dr Honey's research and publications have illuminated the perspectives of people with mental health problems and intellectual disabilities, and she has particular expertise in the role of parenting in health management.

**Dr Desiree Boughtwood, BA (Hons), MA, PhD, Dip Counseling**, is a counselor whose doctorate entitled "Anorexia Nervosa in the Clinic" examined the experiences and interpersonal relationships of teenage girls with anorexia in hospital and presented practical solutions for improving treatment and hospitalization. Dr Boughtwood has also researched and published on the role of the media in anorexia. She has extensive personal experience and insight into eating disorders and has lived for many years with a sister with anorexia.

# References

1. Halse, C. and Honey, A. (2005) 'Unravelling ethics: Illuminating the moral dilemmas of research ethics.' *Signs: Journal of Women in Culture and Society: Special Issue on Dilemmas in Feminist Social Research 30*, 4, 2142–61.

2. Bordo, S. (1993) *Unbearable Weight: Feminism, Western Culture and the Body.* Berkeley: University of California Press.

3. Chernin, K. (1985) *The Hungry Self: Women, Eating and Identity.* New York: Times Books.

4. Fallon, P., Katzman, M.A. and Wooley, S.C. (eds) (1994) *Feminist Perspectives on Eating Disorders.* New York: Guilford Press.

5. Orbach, S. (1986) *Hunger Strike: The Anorectic's Struggle as a Metaphor for Our Age.* London: Faber & Faber.

6. Malson, H. (1998) *The Thin Woman: Feminism, Post-structuralism and the Social Psychology of Anorexia Nervosa.* London: Routledge.

7. American Psychiatric Association (2000) *Diagnostic and Statistical Manual of Mental Disorders, IV-TR.* Washington, DC: American Psychiatric Association.

8. Beumont, P. and Touyz, S. (2003) 'What kind of illness is anorexia nervosa?' *European Child & Adolescent Psychiatry 12*, Supplement 1, 20–4.

9. Polivy, J. and Herman, C.P. (2002) 'Causes of eating disorders.' *Annual Review of Psychology 53*, 187–213.

10. Fichter, M.M., Quadflieg, N. and Hedlund, S. (2006) 'Twelve-year course and outcome predictors of anorexia nervosa.' *International Journal of Eating Disorders 39*, 2, 87–100.

11. Keel, P.K. and Klump, K.L. (2003) 'Are eating disorders culture-bound syndromes? Implications for conceptualizing their etiology.' *Psychological Bulletin 129*, 5, 747–69.

12. Mitchell, J., Cook-Myers, T. and Wonderlich, S. (2005) 'Diagnostic criteria for anorexia nervosa: Looking ahead to DSM-V.' *International Journal of Eating Disorders 37*, Supplement, s95–7.

13. Levine, M. and Smolak, L. (2006) *The Prevention of Eating Problems and Eating Disorders: Theory, Research and Practice.* New Jersey: Lawrence Erlbaum Associates.

14. Cachelin, F.M. and Maher, B.A. (1998) 'Is amenorrhea a critical criterion for anorexia nervosa?' *Journal of Psychosomatic Research 44*, 3–4, 435–40.

15. Watson, T.L. and Anderson, A.E. (2003) 'A critical examination of the amenorrhea and weight criteria for anorexia nervosa.' *Acta Psychiatrica Scandinavica 108*, 175–82.

16. Lee, S., Ho, T.P. and Hsu, L.K. (1993) 'Fat phobic and non-fat phobic anorexia nervosa: A comparative study of 70 Chinese patients in Hong Kong.' *Psychological Medicine 23*, 4, 999–1017.

17. Bemporad, J. (1997) 'Cultural and historical aspects of eating disorders.' *Theoretical Medicine 18*, 401–20.

18. Brumberg, J. (1988) *Fasting Girls: The Emergence of Anorexia Nervosa as a Modern Disease.* Cambridge, MA: Harvard University Press.

19. McClelland, L. and Crisp, A. (2001) 'Anorexia nervosa and social class.' *International Journal of Eating Disorders 29*, 2, 150–6.

20. Gard, M.C.E. and Freeman, C.P. (1996) 'The dismantling of a myth: A review of eating disorders and socio-economic status.' *International Journal of Eating Disorders 20*, 1–12.

21. Becker, A.E. (2004) 'New global perspectives on eating disorders.' *Culture, Medicine and Psychiatry 28*, 4, 433–7.

22. Favaro, A., Ferrara, S. and Santonastaso, P. (2003) 'The spectrum of eating disorders in young women: A prevalence study in a general population sample.' *Psychosomatic Medicine 65*, 701–8.

23. Lewinsohn, P.M., Striegel-Moore, R.H. and Seeley, J.R. (2000) 'Epidemiology and natural course of eating disorders in young women from adolescence to young adulthood.' *Journal of the Academy of Child Adolescent Psychiatry 39*, 1284–92.

24. Wade, T.D., Bergin, J.L., Tiggemann, M., Bulik, C.M. and Fairburn, C.G. (2006) 'Prevalence and long-term course of lifetime eating disorders in an adult Australian twin cohort.' *Australian & New Zealand Journal of Psychiatry 40*, 2, 121–8.

25. Austin, S.B. (2000) 'Prevention research in eating disorders: Theory and new directions.' *Psychological Medicine 30*, 1249–62.

26. Lucas, A.R., Crowson, C.S., O'Fallon, W.M. and Melton, L.J. (1999) 'The ups and downs of anorexia nervosa.' *International Journal of Eating Disorders 26*, 4, 397–405.

27. Schmidt, U. (2003) 'Aetiology of eating disorders in the 21st century: New answers to old questions.' *European Child & Adolescent Psychiatry 12*, Supplement 1, i30–37.

28. Steiner, H., Kwan, W., Shaffer, T.G., Walker, S., Miller, S., Sagar, A. and Lock, J. (2003) 'Risk and protective factors for juvenile eating disorders.' *European Child & Adolescent Psychiatry 12*, Supplement 1, i38–46.

29. Connan, F. and Stanley, S. (2003) 'Biology of appetite and weight regulation.' In J. Treasure, U. Schmidt and E. Van Furth (eds) *Handbook of Eating Disorders.* Chichester: Wiley.

30. Hsu, L. (2001) 'Pathogenesis of anorexia nervosa.' *Hong Kong Journal of Psychiatry 11*, 3, 7–12.

31. Klump, K.L. and Gobrogge, K.L. (2005) 'A review and primer of molecular genetic studies of anorexia nervosa.' *International Journal of Eating Disorders 37*, S43–8.

32. Slof-Op't Landt, M.C.T., van Furth, E.F., Meulenbelt, I., Slagboom, P.E., Bartels, M, Boomsma, D. and Bulik, C.M. (2005) 'Eating disorders: From twin studies to candidate genes and beyond.' *Twin Research and Human Genetics 8*, 5, 467–82.

33. Bulik, C.M. (2005) 'Exploring the gene-environment nexus in eating disorders.' *Journal of Psychiatry & Neuroscience 30*, 5, 335–9.

34. Ghaderi, A. (2001) 'Review of risk factors for eating disorders: Implications for primary prevention and cognitive behavioural therapy.' *Scandinavian Journal of Behaviour Therapy 30*, 2, 57–74.

35. Serpell, L. and Troop, N.A. (2003) 'Psychological factors.' In J. Treasure, U. Schmidt and E. Van Furth (eds) *Handbook of Eating Disorders.* Chichester: Wiley.

36. Cassin, S.E. and von Ranson, K.M. (2005) 'Personality and eating disorders: A decade in review.' *Clinical Psychology Review 25*, 7, 895–916.

37. Klump, K.L., Strober, M., Bulik, C.M., Thornton, L., Johnson, C., Devlin, B., Fichter, M.M., Halmi, K., Kaplan, A.S., Woodside, D.B., Crow, S., Mitchell, J., Rotondo, A., Keel, P.K., Berretini, W.H., Plotnicov, K., Pollice, C., Lilenfeld, L.R. and Kaye, W.H. (2004) 'Personality characteristics of women before and after recovery from an eating disorder.' *Psychological Medicine 34*, 8, 1407–18.

38. Wonderlich, S. (2002) 'Personality and eating disorders.' In C. Fairburn and K. Brownell (eds) *Eating Disorders and Obesity: A Comprehensive Handbook.* New York: Guilford Press.

39. Wonderlich, S.A., Lilenfeld, L.R., Riso, L.P., Engel, S. and Mitchell, J.E. (2005) 'Personality and anorexia nervosa.' *International Journal of Eating Disorders 37*, S68–71.

40. Bruch, H. (1988) *Conversations with Anorexics.* New York: Basic Books.

41. Fairburn, C., Cooper, Z., Doll, H. and Welch, S. (1999) 'Risk factors for anorexia nervosa: Three integrated case-control comparisons.' *Archives of General Psychiatry 56*, 5, 468–476.

42. Becker, H., Koerner, P. and Stoeffler, A. (1981) 'Psychodynamics and therapeutic aspects of anorexia nervosa: A study of family dynamics and prognosis.' *Psychotherapy and Psychosomatics 36*, 1, 8–16.

43. Deluca, K.L. (2000) 'Attachment and sexuality: Comparisons in college women with eating disorder symptoms and those women without eating disorder symptoms.' *Dissertation Abstracts International: Section B: The Sciences and Engineering 60*, 12-B, 6396.

44. Schmidt, U., Tiller, J., Blanchard, M., Andrews, B. and Treasure, J. (1997) 'Is there a specific trauma precipitating anorexia nervosa?' *Psychological Medicine 27*, 3, 523–30.

45. Haudek, C., Rorty, M. and Henker, B. (1999) 'The role of ethnicity and parental bonding in the eating and weight concerns of Asian-American and Caucasian college women.' *International Journal of Eating Disorders 25*, 4, 425–33.

46. Troop, N. (1998) 'Eating disorders as coping strategies: A critique.' *European Eating Disorders Review 6*, 229–37.

47. Wilson, J. (2004) 'Beyond psychiatry: How social workers conceptualise women and self-starvation.' *Australian Social Work 57*, 2, 150–60.

48. Bordo, S. (1993) 'Feminism, Foucault and the politics of the body.' In C. Ramazanoglu (ed.) *Up against Foucault*. London: Routledge.

49. Calam, R. and Slade, P. (1994) 'Eating patterns and unwanted sexual experiences.' In B.M. Dolan and I. Gitzinger (eds) *Why Women? Gender Issues and Eating Problems*. London: Athlone Press.

50. Thompson, B. (1992) '"A way outa no way": Eating problems among African-American, Latina and white women.' *Gender & Society 6*, 4, 546–61.

51. Shelley, R. (1997) *Anorexics on Anorexia*. London: Jessica Kingsley Publishers.

52. Woods, S. (2004) 'Untreated recovery from eating disorders.' *Adolescence 39*, 154, 361–71.

53. Garfinkel, P.E. and Garner, D.M. (1982) *Anorexia Nervosa: A Multidimensional Perspective*. New York: Brunner/Mazel.

54. Ravaldi, C., Vannacci, A., Zucchi, T., Mannucci, E., Cabras, P.L., Boldrini, M., Murciano, L., Rotella, C.M. and Ricca, V. (2003) 'Eating disorders and body image disturbances among ballet dancers, gymnasium users and body builders.' *Psychopathology 36*, 5, 247–54.

55.  Sundgot-Borgen, J., Skarderud, F. and Rodgers, S. (2003) 'Athletes and dancers.' In J. Treasure, U. Schmidt and E. Van Furth (eds) *Handbook of Eating Disorders*. Chichester: Wiley.

56.  Byrne, S. (2002) 'Sport, occupation and eating disorders.' In C. Fairburn and K. Brownell (eds) *Eating Disorders and Obesity: A Comprehensive Handbook*. New York: Guilford Press.

57.  Lawrence, M. (1984) *The Anorexic Experience*. London: Women's Press.

58.  Eliot, A. and Baker, C.W. (2000) 'Maternal stressors and eating-disordered adolescent girls.' *Family Therapy 27*, 3, 165–78.

59.  Haworth-Hoeppner, S. (2000) 'The critical shapes of body image: The role of culture and family in the production of eating disorders.' *Journal of Marriage and the Family 62*, 1, 212–27.

60.  Minuchin, S., Rosman, B.L. and Baker, L. (1978) *Psychosomatic Families: Anorexia Nervosa in Context*. Cambridge, MA: Harvard University Press.

61.  Huline-Dickens, S. (2000) 'Anorexia nervosa: Some connections with the religious attitude.' *British Journal of Medical Psychology 73*, Pt 1, 67–76.

62.  Ward, A., Ramsay, R. and Treasure, J. (2000) 'Attachment research in eating disorders.' *British Journal of Medical Psychology 73*, 1, 35–51.

63.  Tozzi, F., Sullivan, P., Fear, J., McKenzie, J. and Bulik, C.M. (2003) 'Causes and recovery in anorexia nervosa: The patient's perspective.' *International Journal of Eating Disorders 33*, 143–54.

64.  Eisler, I. (1995) 'Family models of eating disorders.' In G. Szmukler, C. Dare and J. Treasure (eds) *Handbook of Eating Disorders: Theory, Treatment and Research*. Chichester: Wiley.

65.  Burggraf, K.K. (2001) 'Eating disorder symptomatology and media, family, psychological and maturational variables: A longitudinal study of young females.' *Dissertation Abstracts International: Section B: The Sciences and Engineering*, 6734.

66.  Steiger, H., Stotland, S., Trottier, J. and Ghadirian, A.M. (1996) 'Familial eating concerns and psychopathological traits: Causal implications of transgenerational effects.' *International Journal of Eating Disorders 19*, 2, 147–57.

67.  Liu, A. (1979) *Solitaire*. New York: Harper and Row.

68.  Paxton, S.J., Schutz, H.K., Wertheim, E.S. and Muir, S.L. (1999) 'Friendship clique and peer influences on body image concerns, dietary restraint, extreme weight-loss behaviors and binge eating in adolescent girls.' *Journal of Abnormal Psychology 108*, 255–66.

69.   Ward, A. and Gowers, S. (2003) 'Attachment and childhood development.' In J. Treasure, U. Schmidt and E. van Furth (eds) *Handbook of Eating Disorders*. Chichester: Wiley.

70.   Larkin, J. and Rice, C. (2005) 'Beyond "healthy eating" and "healthy weights": Harassment and the health curriculum in middle schools.' *Body Image 2*, 3, 219–32.

71.   Lieberman, M., Gauvin, L., Bukowski, W. and White, D. (2001) 'Interpersonal influence and disordered eating in adolescent girls: The role of peer modeling, social reinforcement and body-related teasing.' *Eating Behaviors 2*, 215–36.

72.   Larkin, J., Rice, C. and Russell, V. (1999) 'Sexual harassment and the prevention of eating disorders: Educating young women.' In N. Piran, M.P. Levine and C. Steiner-Adair (eds) *Preventing Eating Disorders: A Handbook of Interventions and Special Challenges*. Philadelphia: Brunner/Mazel.

73.   Liddlelow, E. (2002) 'Fat chances in an anorexic culture.' *Arena 59*, 47–59.

74.   Hornbacher, M. (1998) *Wasted. A Memoir of Anorexia and Bulimia*. New York: HarperCollins.

75.   Thompson, B. (1994) *A Hunger So Wide and So Deep: American Women Speak Out About their Eating Problems*. London: University of Minnesota Press.

76.   Austin, S.B. (2001) 'Population-based prevention of eating disorders: An application of the Rose prevention model.' *Preventative Medicine 32*, 268–83.

77.   Branch, H. and Eurman, L. (1980) 'Social attitudes toward patients with anorexia nervosa.' *American Journal of Psychiatry 137*, 5, 631–32.

78.   Fairburn, C. (2005) 'Evidence-based treatment of anorexia nervosa.' *International Journal of Eating Disorders 37*, Supplement, s26–30.

79.   National Institute for Clinical Excellence (2003) *Eating Disorders: Core Interventions in the Management and Treatment of Anorexia Nervosa, Bulimia Nervosa and Related Eating Disorders*. Leicester: British Psychological Society.

80.   Treasure, J. and Schmidt, U. (2003) 'Treatment overview.' In J. Treasure, U. Schmidt and E. van Furth (eds) *Handbook of Eating Disorders*. Chichester: Wiley.

81.   Winston, A. and Webster, P. (2003) 'Inpatient treatment.' In J. Treasure, U. Schmidt and E. van Furth (eds) *Handbook of Eating Disorders*. Chichester: Wiley.

82. Halse, C., Boughtwood, D., Clarke, S., Honey, A., Kohn, M. and Madden, S. (2005) 'Illuminating multiple perspectives: Meanings of nasogastric feeding in anorexia nervosa.' *European Eating Disorders Review 13*, 4, 264–72.

83. Eisler, I., Dare, C., Russell, G.F.M., Szmukler, G., le Grange, D. and Dodge, E. (1997) 'Family and individual therapy in anorexia nervosa: A 5-year follow-up.' *Archives of General Psychiatry 54*, 11, 1025–30.

84. Shute, J. (1992) *Life-size.* London: Secker & Warburg.

85. Colton, A. and Pistrang, N. (2004) 'Adolescents' experiences of inpatient treatment for anorexia nervosa.' *European Eating Disorders Review 12*, 5, 307–16.

86. Sesan, R. (1994) 'Feminist inpatient treatment for eating disorders: An oxymoron?' In P. Fallon, M. Katzman and S.C. Wooley (eds) *Feminist Perspectives on Eating Disorders.* New York: Guilford Press.

87. Vandereycken, W. (2003) 'The place of inpatient care in the treatment of anorexia nervosa: Questions to be answered.' *International Journal of Eating Disorders 34,* 409–22.

88. Loewenthal, C. (1996) *The Substance from the Shadow.* Sydney: Pen Skill.

89. Robinson, P. (2003) 'Day treatments.' In J. Treasure, U. Schmidt and E. Van Furth (eds) *Handbook of Eating Disorders.* Chichester: Wiley.

90. Zipfel, S., Reas, D., Thornton, C., Olmsted, M., Williamson, D.A., Gerlinghoff, M., Herzog, W. and Beumont, P. (2002) 'Day hospitalization programs for eating disorders: A systematic review of the literature.' *International Journal of Eating Disorders 31*, 2, 105–17.

91. Thornton, C., Beumont, P. and Touyz, S. (2002) 'The Australian experience of day programs for patients with eating disorders.' *International Journal of Eating Disorders 32*, 1, 1–10.

92. Marx, R.D. and Herrin, M. (2005) 'Questions and answers.' *Eating Disorders: The Journal of Treatment & Prevention 13*, 219–22.

93. Dare, C. and Eisler, I. (2002) 'Family therapy and eating disorders.' In C.G. Fairburn and K.D. Brownell (eds) *Eating Disorders and Obesity: A Comprehensive Handbook.* New York: Guilford Press.

94. Lock, J. and Gowers, S. (2005) 'Effective interventions for adolescents with anorexia nervosa.' *Journal of Mental Health 14*, 6, 599–610.

95. Woodside, D.B. (2005) 'Treatment of anorexia nervosa: More questions than answers.' *International Journal of Eating Disorders 37*, Supplement, S41–2.

96. Shafran, R. and de Silva, P. (2003) 'Cognitive behavioural models.' In J. Treasure, U. Schmidt and E. Van Furth (eds) *Handbook of Eating Disorders.* Chichester: Wiley.

97. Wilfley, D., Stein, R. and Welch, R. (2003) 'Interpersonal psychotherapy.' In J. Treasure, U. Schmidt and E. Van Furth (eds) *Handbook of Eating Disorders.* Chichester: Wiley.

98. Morgan, A. (1999) *What is Narrative Therapy? An Easy-to-read Introduction.* Adelaide: Dulwich Centre Publications.

99. Kaplan, A.S. (2002) 'Psychological treatments for anorexia nervosa: A review of published studies and promising new directions.' *Canadian Journal of Psychiatry 47*, 3, 235–42.

100. Richards, P.S., Baldwin, B.M., Frost, H.A., Clark-Sly, J.B., Berrett, M.E. and Hardman, R.K. (2000) 'What works for treating eating disorders? Conclusions of 28 outcome reviews.' *Eating Disorders: The Journal of Treatment and Prevention 8*, 3, 189–206.

101. Zhu, A.J. and Walsh, B.T. (2002) 'Pharmacologic treatment of eating disorders.' *Canadian Journal of Psychiatry 47*, 3, 227–35.

102. Bruna, T. and Fogteloo, J. (2003) 'Drug treatments.' In J. Treasure, U. Schmidt and E. Van Furth (eds) *Handbook of Eating Disorders.* Chichester: Wiley.

103. Noordenbos, G. and Seubring, A. (2006) 'Criteria for recovery from eating disorders according to patients and therapists.' *Eating Disorders: The Journal of Treatment and Prevention 14*, 1, 41–54.

104. Herpertz-Dahlmann, B.M., Wewetzer, C., Schulz, E. and Remschmidt, H. (1996) 'Course and outcome in adolescent anorexia nervosa.' *International Journal of Eating Disorders 19*, 4, 335–45.

105. Lowe, B., Zipfel, S., Buchholz, C., Dupont, Y., Reas, D.L. and Herzog, W. (2001) 'Long-term outcome of anorexia nervosa in a prospective 21-year follow-up study.' *Psychological Medicine 31*, 881–90.

106. Ben-Tovim, D.I. (2003) 'Eating disorders: Outcome, prevention and treatment of eating disorders.' *Current Opinion in Psychiatry 16*, 1, 65–69.

107. Garfinkel, P.E., Moldofsky, H. and Garner, D.M. (1977) 'The outcome of anorexia nervosa: Significance of clinical features, body image and behavior modification.' In R.A. Vigersky (ed.) *Anorexia Nervosa.* New York: Raven Press.

108. Morgan, H.G. and Hayward, A.E. (1988) 'Clinical assessment of anorexia nervosa. The Morgan-Russell outcome assessment schedule.' *British Journal of Psychiatry 152*, 2, 367–71.

109. Steinhausen, H.C., Boyadjieva, S., Giogoroiu-Serbanescu, M. and Neumarker, K.J. (2003) 'The outcome of adolescent eating disorders: Findings from an international collaborative study.' *European Child & Adolescent Psychiatry 12*, Supplement 1, 91–8.

110. Garrett, C. (1998) *Beyond Anorexia: Narrative, Spirituality and Recovery.* Cambridge: Cambridge University Press.

111. Pettersen, G. and Rosenvinge, J. (2002) 'Improvement and recovery from eating disorders: A patient perspective.' *Eating Disorders: The Journal of Treatment and Prevention 10*, 1, 61–71.

112. Weaver, K., Wuest, J. and Ciliska, D. (2005) 'Understanding women's journey of recovering from anorexia nervosa.' *Qualitative Health Research 15*, 2, 188–206.

113. Garrett, C. (1997) 'Recovery from anorexia nervosa: A sociological perspective.' *International Journal of Eating Disorders 21*, 3, 261–72.

114. Fisher, M. (2003) 'The course and outcome of eating disorders in adults and in adolescents: A review.' *Adolescent Medicine 14*, 1, 149–58.

115. Pompili, M., Mancinelli, I., Girardi, P., Ruberto, A. and Tatarelli, R. (2004) 'Suicide in anorexia nervosa: A meta-analysis.' *International Journal of Eating Disorders 36*, 1, 99–103.

116. Steinhausen, H.C. (2002) 'The outcome of anorexia nervosa in the 20th century.' *American Journal of Psychiatry 159*, 8, 1284–93.

117. Hsu, L.K.G. (1996) 'Outcome of early onset anorexia nervosa: What do we know?' *Journal of Youth and Adolescence 25*, 4, 563–8.

118. Bell, L. (2003) 'What can we learn from consumer studies and qualitative research in the treatment of eating disorders?' *Eating & Weight Disorders 8*, 3, 181–7.

119. Keski-Rahkonen, A. and Tozzi, F. (2005) 'The process of recovery in eating disorder sufferers' own words: An internet-based study.' *International Journal of Eating Disorders 37*, Supplement, s80–6.

120. Abraham, S. and Llewellyn-Jones, D. (2001) *Eating Disorders: The Facts*, 5th edn. New York: Oxford University Press.

121. Palmer, B. (2000) *Helping People with Eating Disorders: A Clinical Guide to Assessment and Treatment.* Chichester: Wiley.

122. Williamson, D.A., Gleaves, D.H. and Stewart, T.M. (2005) 'Categorical versus dimensional models of eating disorders: An examination of the evidence.' *International Journal of Eating Disorders 37*, 1, 1–10.

123. Perosa, L.M. and Perosa, S.L. (2004) 'The continuum versus categorical debate on eating disorders: Implications for counselors.' *Journal of Counseling & Development 82*, 203–6.

124. Campos, P. (2004) *The Obesity Myth.* Camberwell, Victoria: Viking.

125. Gordon, R.A. (2000) *Eating Disorders: Anatomy of a Social Epidemic,* 2nd edn. Oxford: Blackwell.

126. Way, K. (1995) 'Never too rich or too thin: The role of stigma in the social construction of anorexia nervosa.' In D. Maurer and J. Sobal (eds) *Eating Agendas.* New York: Walter de Gruyter.

127. Beumont, P. (2000) 'An overview of medical issues related to eating disorders.' In F. Sanders and D. Gaskill (eds) *The Encultured Body: Policy Implications for Healthy Body Image and Disordered Eating Behaviours.* Brisbane: Queensland University Printing and Publications Unit.

128. Atkins, P. and Bowler, I. (2001) *Food in Society.* London: Hodder Headline.

129. Eisler, I., Le Grange, D. and Asen, E. (2003) 'Family interventions.' In J. Treasure, U. Schmidt and E. Van Furth (eds) *Handbook of Eating Disorders.* Chichester: Wiley.

130. American Psychiatric Association Work Group on Eating Disorders (2000) 'Practice guidelines for the treatment of patients with eating disorders (revision).' *American Journal of Psychiatry 157*, Supplement 1, 1–39.

131. Robb, A., Silber, T., Orrell-Valente, J., Ellis, N., Dadson, M. and Chatoor, I. (2002) 'Supplemental nocturnal nasogastric refeeding for better short-term outcomes in hospitalised adolescent girls with anorexia nervosa.' *American Journal of Psychiatry 159*, 8, 1347–53.

132. Mehler, P.S. and Crews, C.K. (2001) 'Refeeding the patient with anorexia nervosa.' *Eating Disorders: The Journal of Treatment and Prevention 9*, 2, 167–71.

133. Zipfel, S., Lowe, B. and Herzog, W. (2003) 'Medical complications.' In J. Treasure, U. Schmidt and E. Van Furth (eds) *Handbook of Eating Disorders.* Chichester: Wiley.

134. Yucel, B., Ozbey, N., Polat, A. and Yager, J. (2005) 'Weight fluctuations during the early refeeding period in anorexia nervosa: Case reports.' *International Journal of Eating Disorders 37*, 175–7.

135. Holtkamp, K., Hebebrand, J. and Herpertz-Dahlmann, B. (2004) 'The contribution of anxiety and food restriction on physical activity in acute anorexia nervosa.' *International Journal of Eating Disorders 36*, 163–71.

136. Boughtwood, D. 'Anorexia nervosa in the clinic: Embodiment, autonomy and shifting subjectivities.' Unpublished PhD thesis. Sydney: University of Western Sydney.

137. Segal, J. 'Listen to our stories: Young women with anorexia nervosa speak out about their hospital experiences.' Unpublished Honours thesis. Sydney: University of New South Wales.

138. Sharpe, D. and Rossiter, L. (2002) 'Siblings of children with a chronic illness: A meta-analysis.' *Journal of Pediatric Psychology 27*, 8, 699–710.

139. Garley, D. and Johnson, B. (1994) 'Siblings and eating disorders: A phenomenological perspective.' *Journal of Psychiatric and Mental Health Nursing 1*, 3, 157–64.

140. Ross, K. and Handy, J.A. (1997) 'Family perceptions of anorexia nervosa: A qualitative study of two families' histories.' In G.M. Habermann (ed.) *Looking Back and Moving Forward: 50 Years of New Zealand Psychology.* Wellington: New Zealand Psychological Society.

141. Howe, G.W. (1993) 'Siblings of children with physical disabilities and chronic illnesses: Studies of risk and social ecology.' In Z. Stoneman and P.W. Berman (eds) *The Effects of Mental Retardation, Disability and Illness on Sibling Relationships: Research Issues and Challenges.* Baltimore: Paul H. Brookes.

142. Taylor, V., Fuggle, P. and Charman, T. (2001) 'Well sibling psychological adjustment to chronic physical disorder in a sibling: How important is maternal awareness of their illness attitudes and perceptions?' *Journal of Child Psychology & Psychiatry & Allied Disciplines 42*, 7, 953–62.

143. Williams, P.D., Williams, A., Graff, C., Hanson, S., Stanton, A., Hafeman, C., Liebergen, A., Leuenberg, K., Setter, R.K., Ridder, L., Curry, H., Barnard, M. and Sanders, S. (2002) 'Interrelationships among variables affecting well siblings and mothers in families of children with a chronic illness or disability.' *Journal of Behavioral Medicine 25*, 5, 411–24.

144. Lobato, D. and Kao, B. (2002) 'Integrated sibling-parent group intervention to improve sibling knowledge and adjustment to chronic illness and disability.' *Journal of Pediatric Psychology 27*, 8, 711–16.

145. Highet, N., Thompson, M. and King, R. (2005) 'The experience of living with a person with an eating disorder: The impact on carers.' *Eating Disorders: The Journal of Treatment and Prevention 13*, 4, 327–44.

146. Honey, A. and Halse, C. (2006) 'The specifics of coping: Parents of daughters with anorexia nervosa.' *Qualitative Health Research 16*, 5, 611–29.

147. Treasure, J., Murphy, T., Szmukler, G., Todd, G., Gavan, K. and Joyce, J. (2001) 'The experience of caregiving for severe mental illness: A comparison between anorexia nervosa and psychosis.' *Social Psychiatry & Psychiatric Epidemiology 36*, 7, 343–7.

148. de la Rie, S., Van Furth, E., Koning, A., Noordenbos, G. and Donker, M. (2005) 'The quality of life of family caregivers of eating disorder patients.' *Eating Disorders: The Journal of Treatment and Prevention 13*, 4, 345–51.

149. Macdonald, M. (1993) 'Bewildered, blamed and broken hearted: Parents' views of anorexia nervosa.' In B. Lask and R. Bryant-Waugh (eds) *Child Onset of Anorexia Nervosa and Related Eating Disorders.* Hove: Psychology Press.

150. Greed, C. (1990) 'The professional and the personal. A study of women quantity surveyors.' In L. Stanley (ed.) *Feminist Praxis. Research, Theory and Epistemology in Feminist Sociology.* London: Routledge.

151. Laws, C.A. (2001) 'Poststructuralism at work with marginalised children.' Unpublished PhD thesis. Sydney: James Cook University.

152. White, M. and Epston, D. (1990) *Narrative Means to Therapeutic Ends.* New York: Norton.

153. Sarason, I.G. and Sarason, B.R. (1993) *Abnormal Psychology: The Problem of Maladaptive Behavior.* Upper Saddle River: Prentice Hall.

154. Monk, G., Winslade, J., Crocket, K. and Epston, D. (1997) *Narrative Therapy In Practice.* San Francisco, CA: Jossey Bass.

155. Bruch, H. (1978) *The Golden Cage: The Enigma of Anorexia Nervosa.* Cambridge, MA: Harvard University Press.

156. Huon, G., Gunewardene, A. and Hayne, A. (2000) 'The gender and SES context of weight-loss dieting among adolescent females.' *Eating Disorders: The Journal of Treatment and Prevention 8*, 2, 147–55.

157. Fear, J.L., Bulik, C.M. and Sullivan, P.F. (1996) 'The prevalence of disordered eating behaviours and attitudes in adolescent girls.' *New Zealand Journal of Psychology 25*, 1, 7–12.

158. Tiggemann, M. (2001) 'Effect of gender composition of school on body concerns in adolescent women.' *International Journal of Eating Disorders 29*, 2, 239–43.

159. Dyer, G. and Tiggemann, M. (1996) 'The effect of school environment on body concerns in adolescent women.' *Sex Roles 34*, 12, 127–38.

160. Mensinger, J. (2001) 'Conflicting gender role prescriptions and disordered eating in single-sex and coeducational school environments.' *Gender and Education 13*, 4, 417–29.

161. Limbert, C. (2001) 'A comparison of female university students from different school backgrounds using the Eating Disorder Inventory.' *International Journal of Adolescent Medicine and Health 13*, 2, 145–54.

162. Cohn, L.D., Adler, N.E., Irwin, C.E., Millstein, S.G., Kegeles, S.M. and Stone, G. (1987) 'Body-figure preferences in male and female adolescents.' *Journal of Abnormal Psychology 96*, 276–9.

163. Halse, C., Honey, A. and Boughtwood, D. (2007) 'The paradox of virtue: (re) thinking deviance, anorexia and schooling.' *Gender and Education 19*, 2, 219–35.

164. Striegel-Moore, R.H., Connor-Greene, P.A. and Shime, S. (1991) 'School milieu characteristics and disordered eating in high school graduates.' *International Journal of Eating Disorders 10*, 2, 187–92.

165. Garner, D.M. and Garfinkel, P.E. (1982) 'Sociocultural factors.' In *Anorexia Nervosa: A Multidimensional Perspective.* Philadelphia: Brunner/Mazel.

166. Levine, M.P. and Piran, N. (2004) 'The role of body image in the prevention of eating disorders.' *Body Image 1*, 1, 57–70.

167. Paxton, S. (1999) 'Peer relations, body image and disordered eating in adolescent girls: Implications for prevention.' In N. Piran, M.P. Levine and C. Steiner-Adair (eds) *Preventing Eating Disorders: A Handbook of Interventions and Special Challenges.* Philadelphia: Brunner/Mazel.

168. Piran, N. (1999) 'The reduction of preoccupation with body weight and shape in schools: A feminist approach.' In N. Piran, M.P. Levine and C. Steiner-Adair (eds) *Preventing Eating Disorders: A Handbook of Interventions and Special Challenges.* Philadelphia: Brunner/Mazel.

169. Pruzinsky, T. and Cash, T. (2004) 'Understanding body image: Historical and contemporary perspectives.' In T. Cash and T. Pruzinsky (eds) *Body Image: A Handbook of Theory, Research and Clinical Practice.* New York: Guilford Press.

170. Garner, D.M. (2004) 'Body image and anorexia nervosa.' In T. Cash and T. Pruzinsky (eds) *Body Image: A Handbook of Theory, Research and Clinical Practice.* New York: Guilford Press.

171. Ogden, J. (2003) *The Psychology of Eating: From Healthy to Disordered Behaviour.* Oxford: Blackwell.

172. Blood, S.K. (2005) *Body Work: The Social Construction of Women's Body Image.* New York: Routledge.

173. Katzman, M.A. and Lee, S. (1997) 'Beyond body image: The integration of feminist and transcultural theories in the understanding of self starvation.' *International Journal of Eating Disorders 22*, 4, 385–94.

174. Mckinley, N.M. (2004) 'Feminist perspectives and objectified body consciousness.' In T. Cash and T. Pruzinsky (eds) *Body Image: A Handbook of Theory, Research and Clinical Practice. New York: Guilford Press.*

175. Vitousek, K., Watson, S. and Wilson, G.T. (1998) 'Enhancing motivation for change in treatment-resistant eating disorders.' *Clinical Psychology Review 18*, 4, 391–420.

176. *Times Educational Supplement* (1999) 'Anorexia? That's a girl's disease.' 16 April, 1–2.

177. Schwitzer, A.M., Bergholz, K., Dore, T. and Salimi, L. (1998) 'Eating disorders among college women: prevention, education, and treatment responses.' *Journal of American College Health 46*, 5, 199–209.

178. Smolak, L. (1999) 'Elementary school curricula for the primary prevention of eating problems.' In N. Piran, M.P. Levine and C. Steiner-Adair (eds) *Preventing Eating Disorders: A Handbook of Interventions and Special Challenges.* Philadelphia: Brunner/Mazel.

179. Tyrka, A.R., Graber, J.A. and Brooks-Gunn, J. (2000) 'The development of disordered eating: Correlates and predictors of eating problems in the context of adolescence.' In A.J. Sameroff, M. Lewis and S. Miller (eds) *Handbook of Developmental Psychopathology*, 2nd edn. New York: Springer.

180. Steiner-Adair, C. (1999) 'Resisting weightism: Media literacy for elementary-school children.' In N. Piran, M.P. Levine and C. Steiner-Adair (eds) *Preventing Eating Disorders: A Handbook of Interventions and Special Challenges.* Philadelphia: Brunner/Mazel.

181. Pratt, B. and Woolfenden, S. (2005) 'Interventions for preventing eating disorders in children and adolescents.' *Cochrane Database of Systematic Reviews 2*, 4.

182. Littleton, H.L. and Ollendick, T. (2003) 'Negative body image and disordered eating behavior in children and adolescents: What places youth at risk and how can these problems be prevented?' *Clinical Child and Family Psychology Review 6*, 1, 51–66.

183. Evans, J., Rich, E. and Holroyd, R. (2004) 'Disordered eating and disordered schooling: What schools do to middle class girls.' *British Journal of Sociology of Education 25*, 2, 123–42.

184. O'Dea, J. and Maloney, D. (2000) 'Preventing eating and body image problems in children and adolescents using the Health Promoting Schools framework.' *Journal of School Health 70*, 1, 18–21.

185. Borresen, R. and Rosenvinge, J. (2003) 'From prevention to health promotion.' In J. Treasure, U. Schmidt and E. Van Furth (eds) *Handbook of Eating Disorders*. Chichester: Wiley.

186. Levine, M.P., Piran, N. and Stoddard, C. (1999) 'Mission more probable: Media literacy, activism, and advocacy as primary prevention.' In N. Piran, M.P. Levine and C. Steiner-Adair (eds) *Preventing Eating Disorders: A Handbook of Interventions and Special Challenges*. Philadelphia: Brunner/Mazel.

187. Nasser, M. and Katzman, M. (1999) 'Eating disorders: Transcultural perspectives inform prevention.' In N. Piran, M.P. Levine and C. Steiner-Adair (eds) *Preventing Eating Disorders: A Handbook of Interventions and Special Challenges*. Philadelphia: Brunner/Mazel.

188. Piran, N., Levine, M.P. and Steiner-Adair, C. (1999) *Preventing Eating Disorders: A Handbook of Interventions and Special Challenges*. Philadelphia: Brunner/Mazel.

189. Langley, J. (2006) *Boys Get Anorexia Too*. London: Sage.

190. Crosscope-Happel, C., Hutchins, D., Getz, H. and Hayes, G. (2000) 'Male anorexia nervosa: A new focus.' *Journal of Mental Health Counseling 22*, 4, 365–70.

191. Muise, A., Stein, D. and Arbess, G. (2003) 'Eating disorder in adolescent boys: A review of the adolescent and young adult literature.' *Journal of Adolescent Health 33*, 6, 427–35.

192. Toro, J., Castro, J., Gila, A. and Pombo, C. (2005) 'Assessment of sociocultural influences on body shape model in adolescent males with anorexia nervosa.' *European Eating Disorders Review 13*, 351–9.

193. Andersen, A.E. (1990) *Males with Eating Disorders*. Philadelphia: Brunner/Mazel.

194. Crisp, A. and collaborators (2006) 'Anorexia nervosa in males: Similarities and differences to anorexia nervosa in females.' *European Eating Disorders Review 14*, 163–7.

195. Bulik, C.M. (2002) 'Anxiety, depression and eating disorders.' In C. Fairburn and K. Brownell (eds) *Eating Disorders and Obesity: A Comprehensive Handbook*. New York: Guilford Press.

196. Wonderlich, S. and Mitchell, J. (1997) 'Eating disorders and comorbidity: Empirical, conceptual, and clinical implications.' *Psychopharmacology Bulletin 33*, 3, 381–90.

197. Gillberg, I.C., Rastam, M. and Gillberg, C. (1995) 'Anorexia nervosa 6 years after onset: Part I. Personality disorders.' *Comprehensive Psychiatry 36,* 1, 61–9.

198. Rastam, M., Gillberg, C. and Gillberg, I.C. (1996) 'A six-year follow-up study of anorexia nervosa subjects with teenage onset.' *Journal of Youth and Adolescence 25,* 4, 439–53.

199. Lock, J. and Le Grange, D. (2005) 'Family-based treatment of eating disorders.' *International Journal of Eating Disorders 37,* Supplement, s64–7.

200. le Grange, D., Binford, R. and Loeb, K.L. (2005) 'Manualized family-based treatment for anorexia nervosa: A case series.' *Journal of the American Academy of Child & Adolescent Psychiatry 44,* 1, 41–6.

201. le Grange, D. (2006) 'How enthusiastic should we be about family-based treatment for adolescent anorexia nervosa?' *European Eating Disorders Review 14,* 6, 373–5.

202. Tierney, S. (2005) 'The treatment of adolescent anorexia nervosa: A qualitative study of the views of parents.' *Eating Disorders: The Journal of Treatment and Prevention 13,* 4, 369–79.

203. Keys, A., Brozek, J., Henschel, A., Mickelson, O. and Taylor, H.L. (1950) *The Biology of Human Starvation.* Minneapolis, MN: University of Minnesota Press.

204. Allen, J. (1991) *Biosphere 2: The Human Experiment.* New York: Viking.

205. Walford, R. (1986) *The 120-year Diet.* New York: Simon & Schuster.

206. Roth, G.S., Ingram, D.K. and Lane, M.A. (2001) 'Caloric restriction in primates and relevance to humans.' *Annals of the New York Academy of Sciences 92,* 302–15.

207. Manke, F.P. and Vitousek, K. (2002) 'Hunger, semistarvation and ill health.' *American Psychologist 57,* 371–2.

208. Polivy, J. (1996) 'Psychological consequences of food restriction.' *Journal of the American Dietetic Association 96,* 6, 589.

209. Vitousek, K. (2004) 'The case for semi-starvation.' *European Eating Disorders Review 12,* 275–8.

210. Vitousek, K., Manke, F.P., Gray, J.A. and Vitousek, M.N. (2004) 'Caloric Restriction for Longevity: II—The systematic neglect of behavioural and psychological outcomes in animal research.' *European Eating Disorders Review 12,* 338–60.

211. Bank, S. and Kahn, M. (1997) *The Sibling Bond.* New York: Basic Books.

212. Cicirelli, V.G. (1995) *Sibling Relationships Across the Lifespan.* New York: Plenum Press.

213. Honey, A., Clarke, S., Halse, C., Kohn, M. and Madden, S. (2006) 'The influence of siblings on the experience of anorexia nervosa for adolescent girls.' *European Eating Disorders Review 14*, 5, 315–22.

214. Honey, A. and Halse, C. (2007) 'Looking after siblings of adolescent girls with anorexia: An important parental role.' *Child: Care, Health and Development 33*, 1, 52–8.

215. Dare, C. and Eisler, I. (1995) 'Family therapy.' In G. Szmukler, C. Dare and J. Treasure (eds) *Handbook of Eating Disorders: Theory, Treatment and Research.* Chichester: Wiley.

216. Lock, J., Le Grange, D., Agras, S. and Dare, C. (2001) *Treatment Manual for Anorexia Nervosa: A Family-based Approach.* New York: Guilford Press.

217. Beale, B., McMaster, R. and Hilege, S. (2004) 'Eating disorders: A qualitative analysis of the parents' journey.' *Contemporary Nurse: A Journal for the Australian Nursing Profession 18*, 1–2, 124–32.

218. Vandereycken, W. and Louwies, I. (2005) '"Parents for Parents:" A self-help project for and by parents of eating disorder patients.' *Eating Disorders 13*, 413–17.

219. Honey, A. and Halse, C. (2005) 'Parents dealing with anorexia nervosa: Actions and meanings.' *Eating Disorders: The Journal of Treatment & Prevention 13*, 4, 353–68.

220. Walkerdine, V., Lucey, H. and Melody, J. (2001) *Growing Up Girl: Psychosocial Explorations of Gender and Class.* Basingstoke: Palgrave.

221. Dixey, R. (1998) 'Healthy eating in schools, overweight and "eating disorders": Are they connected?' *Educational Review 50*, 1, 29–35.

222. Rich, E. and Evans, J. (2005) 'Making sense of eating disorders in schools.' *Discourse: Studies in the Cultural Politics of Education 26*, 2, 247–62.

223. Ampollini, P., Marchesi, C., Gariboldi, S., Cella, P., Peqlizza, C. and Marchesi, C. (1999) 'The Parma high school epidemiological survey: Eating disorders.' *Journal of Adolescent Health 24*, 3, 158–9.

224. Tierney, S. (2006) 'The dangers and draw of online communication: Pro anorexia websites and their implications for users, practitioners and researchers.' *Eating Disorders 14*, 181–90.

225. Rahimi, S. (2003) *Thinner Than Air - A Pro Ana Movement in Cyberspace.* [cited 11 April 2005]; www.alternet.org/story/15058

226. *The Australian* (2001) 'Spare us the skin and bones.' 28 November, 44.

227. Victoria (2004) 'Victoria's pro-ana journal.' [cited 11 April 2005]; www.victoriasproana.com/0main.html

228. Fox, N., Ward, K. and O'Rourke, A. (2005) 'Pro-anorexia, weight-loss drugs and the internet: An "anti-recovery" explanatory model of anorexia.' *Sociology of Health & Illness 27*, 7, 944–71.

229. Pollack, D. (2003) 'Pro-eating disorder websites: What should be the feminist response.' *Feminism and Psychology 13*, 2, 246–51.

230. Shaw, G. (2006) 'Pro anorexia websites: The thin web line.' [cited 10 May 2006]; www.webmd.com/content/Article/109/109381.html

231. *Wave Magazine* (2006) 'The skeleton crew: Inside the pro anorexia movement's underground web campaign'; www.thewavemag.com/pagegen.php? pagename=article&articleid=22888

232. *Time* (2001) 'Anorexia goes high tech.' 12 November, 3.

233. Arndt, L. (2006) *The Anorexic Web* [cited 10 May 2006]; www.anorexicweb.com/InsidetheFridge/proanorexic.html

234. Carney, T., Tait, D., Saunders, D., Touyz, S. and Beumont, P. (2003) 'Institutional options in the management of coercion in anorexia treatment: The antipodean experiment?' *International Journal of Law and Psychiatry 26*, 647–75.

235. Tan, J., Hope, T. and Stewart, A. (2003) 'Competence to refuse treatment in anorexia nervosa.' *International Journal of Law and Psychiatry 26*, 6, 697–707.

236. Keywood, K. (2003) 'Rethinking the anorexic body: How English law and psychiatry "think".' *International Journal of Law and Psychiatry 26*, 599–616.

237. Watson, T., Bowers, W. and Andersen, A. (2000) 'Involuntary treatment of eating disorders.' *American Journal of Psychiatry 157*, 11, 1806–10.

238. Carney, T., Ingvarson, M. and Tait, D. (2004) 'Experiences of "control" in anorexia nervosa treatment: Delayed coercion, shadow of law, or disseminated power and control.' Paper presented at the Societies of Control Conference, Sydney University, Sydney.

239. Gans, M. and Gunn, W. (2003) 'End stage anorexia: Criteria for competence to refuse treatment.' *International Journal of Law and Psychiatry. Anorexia Special Issue 26*, 6, 677–95.

240. Tiller, J., Schmidt, U. and Treasure, J. (1993) 'Compulsory treatment for anorexia nervosa: Compassion or coercion?' *British Journal of Psychiatry 162*, 679–80.

241. Tan, J., Hope, T., Stewart, A. and Fitzpatrick, R. (2003) 'Control and compulsory treatment in anorexia nervosa: The views of patients and parents.' *International Journal of Law and Psychiatry 26*, 627-645.

242. Griffiths, R. and Russell, J. (1998) 'Compulsory treatment of anorexia nervosa patients.' In W. Vandereycken (ed.) *Treating Eating Disorders.* New York: New York University Press.

243. Rathner, G. (1998) 'A plea against compulsory treatment of anorexia nervosa patients.' In W. Vandereycken (ed.) *Treating Eating Disorders.* New York: New York University Press.

244. Neiderman, M., Farley, A., Richardson, J. and Lask, B. (2001) 'Nasogastric feeding in children and adolescents with eating disorders: Towards good practice.' *International Journal of Eating Disorders 29*, 4, 441–8.

245. Carter, J.C., Bewell, C., Blackmore, E. and Woodside, D.B. (2006) 'The impact of childhood sexual abuse in anorexia nervosa.' *Child Abuse & Neglect 30*, 3, 257–69.

246. Purvis, M. and Joyce, A. (2005) 'Child sexual abuse is a global public health problem: Where is Australia?' *Psychiatry, Psychology and Law 12*, 2, 334–44.

247. Thompson, K.M. and Wonderlich, S.A. (2004) 'Child sexual abuse and eating disorders.' In J.K. Thompson (ed.) *Handbook of Eating Disorders and Obesity.* Hoboken, NJ: Wiley.

248. Wonderlich, S.A., Brewerton, T.D., Jocic, Z., Dansky, B.S. and Abbott, D.W. (1997) 'Relationship of childhood sexual abuse and eating disorders.' *Journal of the American Academy of Child and Adolescent Psychiatry 36*, 8, 1107–15.

249. Vize, C.M. and Cooper, P.J. (1995) 'Sexual abuse in patients with eating disorder, patients with depression and normal controls.' *British Journal of Psychiatry 167*, 1, 80–85.

250. Nagata, T., Kiriike, T., Iketani, T., Kawarada, Y. and Tanaka, H. (1999) 'History of childhood sexual or physical abuse in Japanese patients with eating disorders: Relationship with dissociation and impulsive behaviours.' *Psychological Medicine 29*, 4, 935–42.

251. Wentz, E., Gillberg, I.C., Gillberg, C. and Rastam, M. (2005) 'Fertility and history of sexual abuse at 10-year follow-up of adolescent-onset anorexia nervosa.' *International Journal of Eating Disorders 37*, 4, 294–8.

252. Steiger, H. and Zanko, M. (1990) 'Sexual trauma among eating disordered, psychiatric and normal female groups.' *Journal of Interpersonal Violence 5*, 1, 74–86.

253. van Gerko, K., Hughes, M.L., Hamill, M. and Waller, G. (2005) 'Reported childhood sexual abuse and eating-disordered cognitions and behaviors.' *Child Abuse & Neglect 29*, 4, 375–82.

254. Anderson-Fye, E.P. and Becker, A.E. (2004) 'Sociocultural aspects of eating disorders.' In J.K. Thompson (ed.) *Handbook of Eating Disorders and Obesity.* Hoboken, NJ: Wiley.

255. Smolak, L. and Striegel-Moore, R.H. (2001) 'Challenging the myth of the golden girl: Ethnicity and eating disorders.' In R.H. Striegel-Moore and L. Smolak (eds) *Eating Disorders. Innovative Directions in Research and Practice.* Washington, DC: American Psychological Association.

256. Becker, A.E. (2003) 'Eating disorders and social transition.' *Primary Psychiatry 10*, 75–9.

257. Gordon, R.A. (2004) 'Commentary: Towards a clinical ethnography.' *Culture, Medicine and Psychiatry 28*, 4, 603.

258. Katzman, M.A., Hermans, K.M.E., Hoeken, D.V. and Hoek, H.W. (2004) 'Not your "typical island woman": Anorexia nervosa is reported only in subcultures in Curaçao.' *Culture, Medicine and Psychiatry 28*, 4, 463.

259. Rieger, E., Touyz, S.W., Swain, T. and Beumont, P.J. (2001) 'Cross-cultural research on anorexia nervosa: Assumptions regarding the role of body weight.' *International Journal of Eating Disorders 29*, 2, 205–15.

260. Soh, N.L., Touyz, S. and Surgenor, L. (2006) 'Eating and body image disturbances across cultures: A review.' *European Eating Disorders Review 14*, 54–65.

261. Anderson-Fye, E.P. (2004) 'A "Coca-Cola" shape: Cultural change, body image, and eating disorders in San Andrés, Belize.' *Culture, Medicine and Psychiatry 28*, 4, 561.

262. Cummins, L.H., Simmons, A.M. and Zane, N.W.S. (2005) 'Eating disorders in Asian populations: A critique of current approaches to the study of culture, ethnicity, and eating disorders.' *American Journal of Orthopsychiatry 75*, 4, 553.

263. Khandelwal, S.K., Sharan, P. and Saxena, S. (1995) 'Eating disorders: An Indian perspective.' *International Journal of Social Psychiatry 41*, 132–46.

264. Bennett, D., Sharpe, M., Freeman, C. and Carson, A. (2004) 'Anorexia nervosa among female secondary school students in Ghana.' *British Journal of Psychiatry 185*, 4, 312–17.

265. Williamson, L. (1998) 'Eating disorders and the cultural forces behind the drive for thinness: Are African American women really protected?' *Social Work in Health Care 28*, 1, 61-73.

266. le Grange, D., Louw, J., Breen, A. and Katzman, M.A. (2004) 'The meaning of "self-starvation" in impoverished black adolescents in South Africa.' *Culture, Medicine and Psychiatry 28*, 4, 439–61.

267. Desseilles, M., Fuchs, S., Ansseau, M., Lopez, S., Vinckenbosh, E. and Andreoli, A. (2006) 'Achalasia may mimic anorexia nervosa, compulsive eating disorder, and obesity problems.' *Psychosomatics: Journal of Consultation Liaison Psychiatry 47*, 3, 270–1.

268. Lee, S., Wing, Y.K., Chow, C.C., Chung, S. and Yung, C. (1989) 'Gastric outlet obstruction masquerading as anorexia nervosa.' *Journal of Clinical Psychiatry 50*, 5, 184–5.

269. Kaplan, A.S. and Katz, M. (eds) (1993) *Medical Illnesses Associated with Weight Loss and Binge Eating*. Philadelphia: Brunner/Mazel.

270. Ahsanuddin, K.M. and Nyeem, R. (1983) 'Fourth ventricular tumors and anorexia nervosa.' *International Journal of Eating Disorders 2*, 2, 67–72.

271. Gravier, V., Naja, W., Blaise, M. and Cremniter, D. (1998) 'Achalasia and megaesophagus misdiagnosed as anorexia nervosa.' *European Psychiatry 13*, 6, 315–16.

272. Chipkevitch, E. and Fernandes, A.C. (1993) 'Hypothalamic tumor associated with atypical forms of anorexia nervosa and diencephalic syndrome.' *Arquivos de Neuro-Psiquiatría 51*, 2, 270–4.

273. Marshall, J.B. and Russell, J.L. (1993) 'Achalasia mistakenly diagnosed as eating disorder and prompting prolonged psychiatric hospitalization.' *Southern Medical Journal 86*, 12, 1405–7.

274. Pritts, S.D. and Susman, J. (2003) 'Diagnosis of eating disorders in primary care.' *American Family Physician 67*, 2, 297–304.

275. Schellenberg, R. (undated) 'Medical causes of eating disorders – symptoms, treatment, diagnosis' [cited 8 September 2006]; http://randys chellenberg.tripod.com/anorexiatruthinfo/id20.html

276. Vandereycken, W. (1993) 'Misleading variants in the clinical picture of anorexia nervosa.' *European Eating Disorders Review 1*, 3, 183–6.

277. Lupton, D. (1996) *Food, the Body and the Self*. London: Sage.

278. McVeagh, P. (2003) 'Does the media shape our teens?' Paper presented at the Art and Science of Advancing Adolescent Development Conference, Westmead Hospital, Sydney.

279. Wolf, N. (1991) *The Beauty Myth*. London: Chatto & Windus.

280. Allison, D.B., Fontaine, K.R., Manson, J.E., Stevens, J. and Vanitallie, T.B. (1999) 'Annual deaths attributable to obesity in the United States.' *Journal of the American Medical Association 282*, 16, 1530–8.

281. Lee, C.D., Blair, S.N. and Jackson, A.S. (1999) 'Cardiorespiratory fitness, body composition and all-cause and cardiovascular disease mortality in men.' *American Journal of Clinical Nutrition 69*, 373–80.

282. Miller, W.C. (1999) 'Fitness and fatness in relation to health: Implications for a paradigm shift.' *Journal of Social Issues 55*, 2, 207–19.

283. Emsberger, P. and Koletsky, R.J. (1999) 'Biomedical rationale for a wellness approach to obesity: An alternative to a focus on weight loss.' *Journal of Social Issues 55*, 2, 221–60.

284. Gaesser, G. (2002) *Big Fat Lies: The Truth About Your Weight and Your Health.* Carlsbad, CA: Gurze Books.

285. McFarlane, T., Polivy, J. and McCabe, R.E. (1999) 'Help, not harm: Psychological foundation for a nondieting approach toward health.' *Journal of Social Issues 55*, 5, 261–76.

286. Brownell, K.D. and Rodin, J. (1994) 'The dieting maelstrom: Is it possible and advisable to lose weight?' *American Psychologist 49*, 9, 781–91.

287. Garner, D.M. and Wooley, S.C. (1991) 'Confronting the failure of behavioral and dietary treatments for obesity.' *Clinical Psychology Review 11*, 6, 729–80.

288. Berg, F.M. (1999) 'Health risks associated with weight loss and obesity treatment programs.' *Journal of Social Issues 55*, 2, 277–97.

289. Evans, J., Evans, R., Evans, C. and Evans, J.E. (2002) 'Fat free schooling: The discursive production of ill-health.' *International Studies in Sociology of Education 12*, 2, 191–212.

290. Millman, M. (1980) *Such a Pretty Face: Being Fat in America.* New York: Norton.

291. Eivors, A., Button, E., Warner, S. and Turner, K. (2003) 'Understanding the experience of drop-out from treatment for anorexia.' *European Eating Disorders Review 11*, 90–107.

292. Grothaus, K.L. (1998) 'Eating disorders and adolescents: An overview of a maladaptive behavior.' *Journal of Child and Adolescent Psychiatric Nursing 11*, 4, 146 (1).

293. Jarman, M., Smith, J.A. and Walsh, S. (1997) 'The psychological battle for control: A qualitative study of health-care professionals' understandings of the treatment of anorexia nervosa.' *Journal of Community and Applied Social Psychology 7*, 2, 137–52.

294. Kenny, T. (1991) 'Anorexia nervosa: A nursing challenge that can bring results.' *Professional Nurse 6*, 1, 666–9.

295. King, S. and Turner, S. (2000) 'Caring for adolescent females with anorexia nervosa: Registered nurses' perspective.' *Journal of Advanced Nursing 32*, 1, 139–47.

296. Ramjan, L. (2004) 'Nurses and the "therapeutic relationship": Caring for adolescents with anorexia nervosa.' *Journal of Advanced Nursing 45*, 5, 495–503.

297. Brotman, A.W., Stern, T.A. and Herzog, D.B. (1984) 'Emotional reactions of house officers to patients with anorexia nervosa, diabetes and obesity.' *International Journal of Eating Disorders 3*, 4, 71-77.

298. Honey, A., Boughtwood, D., Clarke, S., Halse, C., Kohn, M. and Madden, S. (in press) 'Clinicians supporting parents: Perspectives of parents of adolescents with anorexia.' *Eating Disorders: The Journal of Treatment and Prevention.*

299. Caplan, P.J. and Hall-McCorquodale, I. (1985) 'Mother-blaming in major clinical journals.' *American Journal of Orthopsychiatry 55*, 3, 345–53.

300. Phares, V. (1996) 'Conducting nonsexist research, prevention and treatment with fathers and mothers: A call for change.' *Psychology of Women Quarterly 20*, 55–77.

301. Woollett, A. and Phoenix, A. (1991) 'Psychological views of mothering.' In A. Phoenix, A. Woollett and E. Lloyd (eds) *Motherhood: Meanings, Practices and Ideologies.* London: Sage.

302. Burman, E. (1994) *Deconstructing Developmental Psychology,* 1st edn. London: Routledge.

303. Caplan, P.J. (2000) *The New Don't Blame Mother.* New York: Routledge.

304. Phoenix, A. and Woollett, A. (1991) 'Motherhood: Social construction, politics and psychology.' In A. Phoenix, A. Woollett and E. Lloyd (eds) *Motherhood: Meanings, Practices and Ideologies.* London: Sage.

305. Maine, M. (1993) *Father Hunger: Fathers, Daughters and Food.* London: Simon & Schuster.

306. Fitzgerald, J.F. and Lane, R.C. (2000) 'The role of the father in anorexia.' *Journal of Contemporary Psychotherapy 30*, 1, 71–84.

307. Telerant, A., Kronenberg, J., Rabinovitch, S., Elman, I., Neumann, M. and Gaoni, B. (1992) 'Anorectic family dynamics.' *Journal of the American Academy of Child and Adolescent Psychiatry 31*, 5, 990–1.

308. Sharkey-Orgnero, M.I. (1999) 'Anorexia nervosa: A qualitative analysis of parents' perspectives on recovery.' *Eating Disorders: The Journal of Treatment and Prevention 7*, 2, 123–141.

309. Bryant-Waugh, R. and Lask, B. (1995) 'Eating disorders in children.' *Journal of Child Psychology and Psychiatry and Allied Disciplines 36*, 2, 191–202.

310. Rich, E. (2006) 'Anorexia (dis)connection: Managing anorexia as an illness and an identity.' *Sociology of Health and Illness 28*, 3, 284–305.

311. Nielsen, S. and Bara-Carril, N. (2003) 'Family, burden of care and social consequences.' In J. Treasure, U. Schmidt and E. Van Furth (eds) *Handbook of Eating Disorders*. Chichester: Wiley.

312. Haigh, R. and Treasure, J. (2003) 'Investigating the needs of carers in the area of eating disorders: Development of the Carers' Needs Assessment Measure (CaNAM).' *European Eating Disorders Review 11*, 125–141.

313. Lelwica, M.M. (1999) *Starving for Salvation*. New York: Oxford University Press.

314. Claude-Pierre, P. (1997) *The Secret Language of Eating Disorders*. Moorebank: Bantam.

315. Morgan, J.F., Marsden, P. and Lacey, H. (1999) 'Spiritual starvation?: A case series concerning Christianity and eating disorders.' *International Journal of Eating Disorders 28*, 476–80.

316. Hardman, R.K., Berrett, M.E. and Richards, S.P. (2003) 'Spirituality and ten false beliefs and pursuits of women with eating disorders: Implications for counsellors.' *Counselling and Values 40*, 67–78.

317. Smith, F.T., Hardman, R.K., Richards, P.S. and Fischer, L. (2003) 'Intrinsic religiousness and spiritual wellbeing as predictors of treatment outcome among women with eating disorders.' *Eating Disorders 11*, 15–26.

318. Garrett, C. (1988) *Beyond Anorexia: Narrative, Spirituality and Recovery*. Cambridge: Cambridge University Press.

319. Freedman, R. (1986) *Beauty Bound*. Lexington: Lexington Books.

320. Gaitz, G. and Clearly, S. (2004) 'What a waste.' *60 Minutes*, CBS: Australia.

321. *Cosmopolitan* (2004) 'My phobia of food nearly killed me.' April, 151–2.

322. Mclinton, B. (2002) *Anorexia's Fallen Angel*. Toronto: HarperCollins.

323. Touyz, S. (2005) 'Modern musings on anorexia and bulimia nervosa.' Paper presented at the Education Seminar, Sydney University, Sydney.

324. Bishop, R. (2001) 'The pursuit of perfection: A narrative analysis of how women's magazines cover eating disorders.' *Howard Journal of Communication 12*, 4, 221–40.

325. Way, K. (1993) *Anorexia Nervosa and Recovery: A Hunger for Meaning.* Binghampton, NY: Howarth Press.

326. Boughtwood, D. (2005) 'View to be thin: Interrogating media's relationship to eating disorder through audience research.' *Participations 1*, 3; www.participations.org/volume%201/issue%203/1_03_boughtwood_article.htm (accessed 24 September 2007).

327. Smolak, L. and Murnen, S. (2001) 'Gender and eating problems.' In R.H. Striegel-Moore and L. Smolak (eds) *Eating Disorders. Innovative Directions in Research and Practice.* Washington, DC: American Psychological Association.

328. Rieger, E. and Touyz, S. (2006) 'An investigation of the factorial structure of motivation to recover in anorexia nervosa using the Anorexia Nervosa Stages of Change Questionnaire.' *European Eating Disorders Review 14*, 4, 269–75.

329. DiClemente, C.C. and Prochaska, J.O. (1998) 'Toward a comprehensive, transtheoretical model of change: Stages of change and addictive behaviors.' In W.R. Miller and N. Heather (eds) *Treating Addictive Behaviours.* New York: Plenum Press.

330. Prochaska, J.O. and DiClemente, C.C. (1982) 'Transtheoretical therapy: Toward a more integrative model of change.' *Psychotherapy: Theory, Research and Practice 19*, 276–88.

331. Touyz, S., Thornton, C., Rieger, E., George, L. and Beumont, P. (2003) 'The incorporation of the stage of change model in the day hospital treatment of patients with anorexia nervosa.' *European Child & Adolescent Psychiatry 12*, Supplement 1, 65–71.

332. Treasure, J. and Bauer, B. (2003) 'Assessment and motivation.' In J. Treasure, U. Schmidt and E. Van Furth (eds) *Handbook of Eating Disorders.* Chichester: Wiley.

333. Davidson, R. (1998) 'The transtheoretical model: A critical overview.' In W.R. Miller and N. Heather (eds) *Treating Addictive Behaviors.* New York: Plenum Press.

334. Wilson, G.T. and Schlam, T.R. (2004) 'The transtheoretical model and motivational interviewing in the treatment of eating and weight disorders.' *Clinical Psychology Review 24*, 3, 361–78.

335. Hasler, G., Delsignore, A., Milos, G., Budderberg, C. and Schnyder, U. (2004) 'Application of Prochaska's transtheoretical model of change to patients with eating disorders.' *Journal of Psychosomatic Research 57*, 1, 67–72.

336. Treasure, J. and Schmidt, U. (2001) 'Ready, willing and able to change: Motivational aspects of the assessment and treatment of eating disorders.' *European Eating Disorders Review 9*, 1, 4–18.

337. Miller, W.R. and Rollnick, S. (1991) *Motivational Interviewing: Preparing People for Change*. New York: Guilford Press.

# Index